PLAYS FROM
BLACK AUSTRALIA

Jack Davis

Eva Johnson

Richard Walley

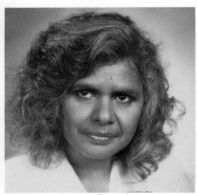

Justine Saunders

Bob Maza

PLAYS FROM BLACK AUSTRALIA

Jack Davis
Eva Johnson
Richard Walley
Bob Maza

With an introduction by
Justine Saunders

CURRENCY PRESS • SYDNEY

Love to LCN — JS

CURRENCY PLAYS
General Editor: Katharine Brisbane

First published in 1989 by
Currency Press Pty. Ltd.,
P.O. Box 452 Paddington, N.S.W. 2021.
Australia.

Reprinted 1992, 1995, 1997

National Library of Australia
Cataloguing-in-Publication data
ISBN 0 86819 226 0

    1. Australian drama — 20th century. 2. Aborigines,
    Australian — Drama.

A822'.308089915

Typeset and printed by Southwood Press
Cover design by Trevor Hood
Cover illustration reproduced by kind permission
    of Jimmy Pike.

Arts for
Australians
Australia Council

Currency's creative writing program
assisted by the Australia Council, the
Federal Government's arts funding and
advisory body.

Contents

Introduction

Justine Saunders

Storytelling has always been a part of our Aboriginal heritage, not just for entertainment, but an essential part of passing down the law and lineage of each group. Whether we live in the bush or in the cities, without our culture and heritage we would shrivel up and die. It is the lifeblood that flows in us and sustains us.

The expression of my culture is through the arts, something that has been passed down to me through my people, listening to my mum, aunties and uncles telling Dreamtime stories. I look forward to passing the stories on to those who come after me. I've always believed that through the arts, performing or visual, you can educate and entertain those who don't understand the Aboriginal way of life.

Aboriginal culture contains all the dramatic elements that Western theatre demands, but since the coming of the white man two hundred years ago, that part of our heritage has been under attack and the tribal way has been eroded. Under the pressure of European culture and arts, merely to be heard we have had to adopt or adapt European art forms. With theatre, the first steps towards telling our stories our way have been taken fairly recently. It is interesting that the early Aboriginal plays were written in prison and theatre was used as a forum for protest. The first play, *The Cherry Pickers* by Kevin Gilbert, was written in 1968 and in the 1970s The Black Theatre

Company was formed and out of it came *The Cake Man* by Robert Merritt. *The Cake Man* was extraordinarily successful from the time it was first workshopped to its U.S.A. premiere at the World Theatre Festival in Denver, Colorado, in 1982. However, the Black Theatre didn't continue. For a time it looked as though an Aboriginal viewpoint in Australian theatre was doomed to be transient, but now in the late 1980s the situation has changed greatly, due in large part to the success of one playwright, Jack Davis.

'We have survived' was the Aboriginal message to white Australians celebrating their bicentenary in 1988. It is a message that runs through all of Jack Davis's work. He is saying that despite what has happened to our people since the dregs of Britain were first dumped on our land in 1788, we are still here. *The Dreamers* is a typical example of his work. Through the Wallitch family, he shows that despite bad health, disillusionment and excessive drinking, Aborigines are surviving, and that is in itself an achievement. *The Dreamers* also addresses the central problem of how to survive with an Aboriginal sense of identity, as Worru puts it:

> Now we who were there
> who were young
> are now old and live in suburbia
> and my longing is an echo
> a re-occurring dream
> coming back along the track
> from where bushfires used to gleam

How, then, to reconcile a way of life tied to being a part of the land, whilst living in suburbia? This conflict is also visible in Jack's writing style which is a mixture of social realism, and the anti-naturalistic style he uses to represent the Dreamtime world. He never really resolves the two, because you can't; just as you can't go back to a traditional way of life, nor can you live a totally European way, with its alien spirituality. No, the way ahead is to try and keep what's good of the past, its sense of community and extended family, and to try and keep our languages alive and make the children feel proud of their heritage. Dolly is a wonderful Jack Davis heroine. She will make sure that Meena and Shane finish school, money or no money, and it's through her and Uncle Worru and the rest of the Wallitch family that we know that despite poverty, deaths in custody, bad health and white hatred, the *Nyoongah* spirit will survive.

Coordah tells the story of the Western Australian *Nyoongah* people through Treb, his wife Elly, their family and friends. Written by Richard Walley, another West Australian, it was workshopped at the First National Black Playwrights Conference held in January 1987. The Conference was the brainchild of noted Aboriginal actor and director, Brian Syron, who worked tirelessly to try and realise his vision of an Aboriginal theatre. *Coordah* went on to have its premiere in Perth, West Australia, later in 1987.

There is something very different about acting in a play written and directed by Black Australians, compared to acting in a play written and directed by whites. For a start, you don't have to explain things to the other black actors. We know what it is like living in white Australia. We are also much more forgiving to our people as characters. Whites have a tendency to make moral judgements or use us as vehicles for messages, rather than treating us as people. In *Coordah* Walley makes no attempt to gloss over the problems in Aboriginal society. Yes, he says, there is drunkeness and aggression, but there is also humour, wonderful humour born of the breadline, and a sense of the real worth of everyone no matter how down and out. One of the great achievements is the character Nummy. Written by a white he would come across as a drunken no-hoper. Richard Walley has created a full character: a liar, a drunkard, a braggart and sexual daydreamer but somebody who, although he may seem down and out, is also full of life and humanity. He is not a cartoon or cipher, but a real human being.

Like Jack Davis, Richard Walley is saying we must fight the overwhelming influence of European culture. One of the most devastating lines in the play is when Jillawarra says to the white manager, Davis, 'You people have removed our thinking'. The wonderful thing about being in a play like *Coordah* is that for those of us performing it and other Black Australians watching it, this play is another step towards regaining our thinking.

Eva Johnson is one of our new playwrights. Like Jack Davis, she came to the theatre through poetry and *Murras* was workshopped at the First National Black Playwrights Conference. This play about three generations of women, is fuelled by a great anger at the injustices the Aboriginal people have suffered. Unlike the three other plays in this collection, this is specifically about Black women. If at times this short play seems to have too many incidents, too many things going on, that can be read as a reflection of all that has happened to us in two hundred years, contrasting with the 60,000 years we were part of this land and of our own culture. If at times the facts seem sensational — the taking of babies from their mothers, the secret sterilisation of Black girls, the fact that we were only made citizens of our own country in 1967 — then think again. Each is horrifyingly true. Although Eva Johnson has Grandmother refer back to the past, as Worru does in *Dreamers*, she sees the past in a different political context to Jack Davis. Although she is saying that the family is important to keep the Aboriginal spirit alive and flourishing, she is also saying that the Aboriginal identity has to be fought for. As I said earlier, the play is fuelled by a great anger, and that anger has been necessary for us to make our voice heard.

The Keepers is based on the true story of the Smiths, a Scottish family who arrived in the Rivoli Bay area of South Australia in the 1840s, and their meeting with the last remaining Boandik people. They became friends and the Smiths documented a history of the Boandik. When the Smiths shifted to Mount Gambier in the 1860s, they took with them the last remnants of the tribe. They set up a house, *Clarendon*, for young Aboriginal girls to be trained in domestic sciences.

If the Smith's actions seem condescending, for the times they were an enlightened couple.

Bob Maza's play has a different epic sense to the other three, in both the time span and in the interplay between the black and white couples. He is saying that there is a possibility of reconciliation between the two cultures and the two peoples. At times *The Keepers* is very moving in the way it shows how it hasn't always been white aggression, but sometimes white ignorance that has helped to destroy tribal culture and beliefs. When the play was produced in Sydney in 1988, it was also important on another level. It was the first play produced by the Aboriginal National Theatre Trust, an all-Aboriginal production company, and it gave us a sense that Black Theatre in Australia was going to get stronger.

There are many new and wonderful plays being written, and we are telling our side of the story. They, like the four plays in this collection, are only the starting point of the many stories we have to tell from the Dreamtime to now.

Sydney, February, 1989

Love to LCN — JS

THE DREAMERS

Michael Fuller as the Dancer, Swan River Stage Company production. Photo: Mike Aitken.

Lynette Narkle as Dolly, Jack Davis as Worru, National Theatre
Company tour 1983. Photo: Geoffrey Lovell.

The Dreamers was first performed by the Swan River Stage Company at the Dolphin Theatre, Perth, on 2 February 1982 with the following cast:

WORRU	Jack Davis
DOLLY	Lynette Narkle
MEENA	Maxine Narkle
SHANE	John Pell
ROY	Michael Fuller
ELI	Trevor Parfitt
PETER	Luke Fuller
DARREN	Shane McIntyre
ROBERT	Wayne Bynder
DANCER	Michael T. Fuller

Didgeridoo music played by Richard Walley

Lighting and set design by Keith Edmundson
Choreography by Richard Walley
Directed by Andrew Ross

CHARACTERS

UNCLE WORRU, an old Aboriginal
DOLLY, his niece
MEENA, her daughter, aged fourteen
SHANE, her son, aged twelve
ROY, her husband
ELI, a cousin
PETER, her son, aged eighteen
DARREN, a white boy, about twelve years old
ROBERT, Dolly's nephew
A tribal dancer

SETTING

The action takes place over six months in the home of the Wallitch family, in South-Western Australia.
The time is the present.

ACT ONE

BEERUK — SUMMER

SCENE ONE

Dawn. We hear the distant echoing voices of children singing a tribal song.

A tribal family walks slowly across the escarpment silhouetted against the first light of dawn. The men lead, carrying weapons, the women and children follow with bags, kulumans *and fire sticks. As they disappear the voices fade and a narrow beam of light reveals* WORRU *alone downstage.*

WORRU:

> I walked down the track
> to where the camp place used to be
> and voices, laughing, singing
> came surging back to me.
>
> It was situated on the Swan
> not far from the old homestead.
> That's gone too.
> Kindly old man Hammersley,
> they can stay there as long as they like,
> he said.
> Now he too is dead.
> Billy Kimberley used to corroboree
> there weekends
> for a tin of Lucky Hit,
> then share it with his friends.
>
> Now we who were there
> who were young,
> are now old and live in suburbia,
> and my longing is an echo
> a re-occurring dream,
> coming back along the track
> from where the campfires used to gleam.

Then there was Angie,
twenty-two stone.
Proud she and Herbie was proper given
church married not livin'.
Meal times,
Bella pulling the damper like a golden moon
from the ashes of the fire,
then sharing the last of the bacca,
some with clay pipes
and others rolling.

Now we who were there
who were young,
are now old and live in suburbia,
and my longing is an echo
a re-occurring dream,
coming back along the track
from where the campfires used to gleam.

[*The spotlight on* WORRU *fades.*]

SCENE TWO

Early morning — a hot, still summer morning. The sound of warbling magpies and children.

In the living room ROY *sits lethargically reading the paper.* COUSIN ELI *is pencilling selections on the racing page while* DOLLY *prepares bread, butter and tea for breakfast. A large battered saucepan of water begins to boil on the stove. Eventually* DOLLY *peers into it and calls out in a piercing voice.*

DOLLY: Come on, you kids. Hurry up, water's ready.
MEENA: I'm having it first.
    [MEENA *and* SHANE *enter arguing.*]
SHANE: No you're not, I am.
MEENA: I am! You can have it after.

SHANE: [*pushing past* MEENA] You didn't wash before breakfast, you might as well go to school without one.

MEENA: Listen who's talkin', when you wash you don't even get wet anyhow.

SHANE: I do so.

MEENA: You might as well use spit.

[MEENA *grabs the saucepan off the stove and* SHANE *pushes her. Water splashes onto the floor.*]

[*running off with the saucepan*] Watch it, Shane.

SHANE: [*chasing her*] You're spilling it all.

[MEENA *and* SHANE *exit.*]

DOLLY: You two be careful.

MEENA: [*off*] Was Shane's fault.

DOLLY: Shut yer trap both of yer —

SHANE: [*off*] 'S her fault —

DOLLY: — and share the water.

[DOLLY *places a mug of tea and some buttered bread in front of* ROY. *The commotion continues offstage.*]

SHANE: Save some for me.

MEENA: All right.

SHANE: Don't use it all, like you always do.

MEENA: I'm not, get out of the road.

SHANE: Mum said you gotta share it.

MEENA: Yeah, well give us the soap.

SHANE: You're using it all.

MEENA: Ma-a-am, Shane won't gimme the soap.

SHANE: All right, here ya are. Give us some water.

MEENA: Careful, Shane.

SHANE: Watch it!

[*The sound of screaming, the saucepan crashing to the floor.* DOLLY *rushes out after them,* ROY *looks up from his paper.*]

DOLLY: Oh, gawd! What happened?

MEENA: I had it first.

SHANE: She wouldn't leave me any.

DOLLY: You're lucky you never burnt yourselves.

SHANE: It wasn't my fault.

DOLLY: [*returning*] All right, you can wash in cold water now and you can mop up the mess. [*To* ROY] Oh Gawd,

I wish we 'ad a decent place to live in. No hot water,
no locks on the doors, worse than livin' in a bloody
camp.

[ROY *retreats into the newspaper.*]

Why don't you go down the Road Board? They'd put
you on. Cousin William got a job there.

[MEENA *enters, saunters across the room and collects a
balding mop. She exits.*]

They've even got a *Nyoongah* bloke drivin' the garbage
truck.

ELI: Yeah, an' they do all right sellin' bottles an' things,
'sides their wages.

ROY: Well, why don't you go down an' see 'em for a job,
then?

ELI: For me or for you Unc?

DOLLY: [*to* ROY] You? If you weren't so bloody bone tired
we'd get a good 'ouse an' good furniture.

MEENA: [*off*] Give it to me!

SHANE: [*off*] No!

MEENA: [*off*] I had it first.

[MEENA *appears at the door.*]

Mum, Shane won't give me the comb. Mum, make
him give it to me.

DOLLY: Shane, give it to her and shut up, the both of
you.

[SHANE *enters pushing roughly past* MEENA.]

SHANE: All right, then I won't comb my hair.

[*He hurls the comb at* MEENA.]

You can keep your stinkin' old comb.

DOLLY: Oh, what difference does it make? You can still
use it after.

SHANE: What, after her? Don't want none of her nits.

ELI: [*producing a comb*] 'Ere, use mine.

[SHANE *painfully combs the knots out of his hair.*]

You oughta get it cut, you're startin' to look like a
yorga.

SHANE: Shut yer mouth, cousin Eli, you're only jealous
'cause you look like a fuzzy mop walking down the
street. Wonder the cops don't turn you upside down

and use you for a mop down the lock up on a Sunday morning.

DOLLY: That'll do, that's enough.

[SHANE *throws the comb to* ELI, *grabs several slices of bread and slouches off.*]

You shut up, Eli, an' think about washin' yourself. I want you to come down the 'ospital with me to pick up Uncle Worru.

ELI: Aw, come on Aunty, I had trouble with me eye all night.

ROY: Urgh! Eye, me *kwon*.

DOLLY: Ah, don't worry about it. I'll go on me own. [*Pointing to* ROY] I can see you're related to 'im.

MEENA: [*entering neat and tidy, school bag in hand*] Mum, that isn't a *Nyoongah* driving the garbage truck, 'es an Indian bloke.

DOLLY: What of it, still coloured, ain't he?

ROY: Lot of difference, he ain't a *Nyoongah* an that's good enough for me.

[PETER *enters, ambling across the front of the stage.*]

MEENA: [*imperiously*] As a matter of fact there's very little difference. They are very much like Aborigines because that's where we come from, India. We came across the land bridge, then the sea came behind us and Australia was iso . . . isolated and the only animal we brought with us was the dingo.

DOLLY: All right, Miss *Wetjala*, git goin' to school.

[MEENA *leaves, pulling* ELI's *hair.*]

MEENA: 'Bye, fuzzy top, 'bye.

[MEENA *leaves, but returns to the doorway.*]

Peter's comin'.

[MEENA *exits.*]

DOLLY: [*pointing at* ROY] You wanna check that boy.

ROY: Aw, 'es old enough to look after 'imself.

[PETER *appears in the doorway.*]

Where d'you git to last night?

PETER: Aw, I stopped out at Aunty Peggy's.

ELI: [*grinning*] *Bunjin'* around, I bet.

PETER: You're only jealous, anyway.

DOLLY: You sure you was at Aunty Peggy's?

PETER: Yeah, course I was.

DOLLY: Well 'ow d'ya git 'ere?

PETER: She gave me a bus fare.

DOLLY: Next time you stay out, you let me know.

PETER: OK.

ELI: [*miming handcuffs*] I thought you was *woonana*.
    [DOLLY *pours him a cup of tea.*]

PETER: Was you afraid I mighta 'ad your favourite cell?

ELI: [*laughing*] Which one's that?

ROY: He's got his name scratched in all of 'em.

ELI: Yeah, Sergeant thought about puttin' a brass name
    plate on the door for me; Elijah William Zakariah
    Wallitch.

ROY: Jacky, you mean.

ELI: Yeah, Elijah William Zakariah Wallitch, Jacky.
    [*They laugh.*]

DOLLY: And how's Aunty Peggy?

PETER: Aw, she's all right.

DOLLY: The boy 's 'ome?

PETER: Yeah, Big mob there, Northam lot came down
    Friday, they was still there when I left.

ROY: Hope they don't come round lookin' for *boondah*
    for petrol to git 'ome.

ELI: [*smacking his pockets*] Won't be gettin' any *boondah*
    out of me. [*Gesturing nothing*] 'Cause I'm like that.

PETER: Don't you know how to milk a bowser?

ELI: [*shrugging his shoulders*] Nah.

ROY: [*feigning surprise*] Oh Eli, now, that's hard to believe.

PETER: It's easy, all you gotta do is pick the lock, then
    you gotta switch —

DOLLY: [*interrupting, flicking him*] That'll do from you. If
    you wanta pick anythin' you can come down with me
    an' pick up Uncle Worru.

PETER: Aw, Mum, I'm feeling a bit tired. Those fellas
    kept me awake all night talkin' an' playin' cards. Gawd,
    they're a rowdy lot.

DOLLY: If you'd come home, you'd a gotta decent sleep.

[DOLLY *slams a handful of money on the table and addresses* ROY.]

An' you can go down the butcher an' git some flaps an' bread an' 'ave it cooked for the kids at lunchtime. I'm goin' to pick up Uncle Worru and send him home in a taxi. An' you two clean up, an' clean up properly.

[ROY *produces cigarette butts and breaks them open for tobacco.*]

ROY: 'Ow about some *gnummari*?

DOLLY: Get yourself a job and you'll have plenty a smokes.

ROY: Aw, come on love. Gimme another forty cents an' I'll 'ave enough for a packet.

DOLLY: You got enough here for papers; it won't hurt you to pick up a few butts, an' it won't be the first time.

ROY: An' it won't be the bloody last.

[*They sit in silence.* DOLLY *walks purposefully across the stage and exits.* ROY *finds a longish butt, attempts to light up and lets out a deep hacking chest cough.*]

ELI: Well, what's on the programme for today?

[*Silence.*]

Anybody got any ideas?

[*Silence.*]

How about a bottle of *gnoop*?

ROY: Bloody good idea. Take this cough off me chest.

ELI: [*looking at the money*] If we 'ad some *boondah*?

ROY: No *choo*. Can't use this, gotta git tucker.

ELI: Plenty time to scrounge for tucker, it's early yet, sun just up in the air. Don't worry, ol' Hawkeye'll 'ave some money by lunchtime.

[*They look at each other guiltily until* ROY *finally throws the money in the centre of the table.*]

ROY: All right, who's goin' to go?

PETER: Well, I'm not goin' to the Exchange, anyway.

ELI: Why not?

PETER: Fuckin' barman put me outa there last night.

ROY: What? You got as much right as anybody else.

ELI: What for?

PETER: Aw, he reckon I king hit that *Wetjala* bloke in the
  goonamia Friday night.
ELI: What bloke?
PETER: You know that big ding bloke with the bendy
  back?
ELI: That bloke. He's always hangin' around *Nyoongah*
  yorgas, he's only a gin tailer. Fancy refusin' a man a
  drink over scum like him; bastard deserved all he got.
PETER: Yeah, an' I give it to him, flattened him, [*miming*
  a heavy punch] bukily. Put 'im right down in the *koomp*.
ROY: [*miming handcuffs*] You wanna watch it.
PETER: All right, gimme the money.
  [PETER *collects the money and swaggers towards the door.*]
ROY: You better keep away from the Exchange.
PETER: Yeah, I'll go to the grog shop.
ELI: [*calling*] Git port.
  [PETER *walks across the stage counting the money.*]
ROY: And don't forget cigarette papers.
ELI: And some butts.
  [*The lights fade as* PETER *exits.*]

SCENE THREE

A distant ambulance siren, the hollow footsteps and clatter of
a hospital corridor.

A pool of light reveals WORRU, *dressed in a second-hand*
suit, but without shoes, sitting awkwardly on a hospital bed. An
old suitcase stands at the end of the bed. Eventually DOLLY
enters.

DOLLY: 'Ullo Uncle Worru. [*Kissing him*] I come to get
  you. You ready to come 'ome?
WORRU: Yeah, where you bin? I bin waitin' all mornin'
  for you.
DOLLY: Sorry Uncle, I got 'ere quick as I could. Eh, where
  d'ya get your new clothes from?

WORRU: Sister give 'em to me; she get 'em from Red Cross.

[*He shows off a new white handkerchief.*]

DOLLY: And new 'anky.

WORRU: New sockses too; pretty ones.

DOLLY: Where's your shoes?

[WORRU *points under the bed.*]

WORRU: There somewheres.

[*He bends down and almost topples off the bed.*]

DOLLY: Woops, careful, careful, you gonna look like a real *bridaira*. Lift your foot up. [*Putting on his shoes*] They won't know you when you get home.

WORRU: Who's 'ome?

DOLLY: Oh, just our lot, they all sittin' around like that.

[DOLLY *indicates they are broke, by making a circle with her thumb and index finger.*]

WORRU: What, Eli got *boondah*?

DOLLY: No, he's *koorawoorliny*.

WORRU: *Koorawoorliny*, what's wrong with ol' Hawkeye?

DOLLY: He's got 'em, 'e goes for the big kill Thursdays, late night shopping. Stand up now, Unc, see if your shoes are all right.

[WORRU *stands up and flicks imaginary dust off his clothes with his handkerchief.* DOLLY *straightens his clothes.*]

Right, where's your bag?

[*He points, she picks it up and looks inside.*]

You got your old clothes in here. What's this?

[*She holds up a slice of toast.*]

WORRU: Toast. I save from breakfast.

DOLLY: [*laughing*] What for?

WORRU: I allus git *kobble weert* 'fore lunchtime.

DOLLY: Uncle Worru! Now you feel all right to walk home?

WORRU: *Kia*, I feel good.

DOLLY: No-o-oh. I think I betta get a taxi for you. I gotta go and pay the rent.

WORRU: [*stamping his feet*] No, I wanna *tjen kooliny*, stretch my *marta*. I'm *moorditj*.

DOLLY: No, taxi for you, old fella. You gotta stay *moorditj*. No more drink for you, or you be right back 'ere in this bed again.

WORRU: No, not comin' back 'ere. Next time I go to *Nyoongah* doctor, *boolyaduk*, Pinjarra. Get too many needles in this place. They no good, *warrah*.

DOLLY: Well, you ready? We gotta go an see sister now before you leave.

WORRU: You go, I wait out 'ere.

DOLLY: No, Unc. Sister wants to talk to you, tell you about your medicine, and comin' back for a check up.

WORRU: No, not comin' back 'ere.

DOLLY: [*laughing*] Why don't you want to see her? She's been real nice to you.

[WORRU *shakes his head.*]

Why don't you wanna see her?

WORRU: She might wanna give me 'nother needle.

DOLLY: [*laughing*] Oh, come on, Unc, you're finish with them now.

WORRU: I go this way.

[*He moves away, but* DOLLY *steers him back the other way.*]

DOLLY: Come on, Unc, steady, steady, walk *dubbakyny* now.

[DOLLY *gently shepherds* WORRU *off.*]

WORRU: Needles, needles. [*Pointing to his arms*] In 'ere, in 'ere [*pointing to his side*] an' in there; [*pointing to his posterior*] an' in there. I feel like a bloody *nyngarn*.

[*They exit.*]

SCENE FOUR

The hospital sounds give way to a noisy argument as light builds on the kitchen area.

    PETER, ROY, WORRU *and* ELI *sit around the table drinking. Two bottles stand on the table, one empty, the other full.*

ELI: [*shouting*] Freeo? What's wrong with Fremantle Gaol?

PETER: What's wrong with it?

ELI: You git three meals a day and a hot shower. Not like this place.

ROY: Ay, an' how you gunna git on for a drink?

ELI: Yuh can git a boot polish cocktail now and again.

ROY: You and your boot polish cocktail, bloody paint thinners. That's what killing those stupid black bastards down there, not what they're gittin' 'round the back.

ELI: Bullshit! I still reckon they knocked old Sandy off and dumped him back in the cell. Look you blokes, I'm tellin' yuh, Sandy was as tough as an old boomer. Slept under bridges, ate 'ard tucker all 'is life. Heart failure, be buggered; number nines killed 'im, that's for sure.

PETER: OK, number nines knocked him off. But how you gonna prove it?

ELI: You can't prove nothin', 'cause them screws are too bloody smart for dumb blackfellas.

PETER: It's not because they're too smart, there's just too bloody many of them.

ROY: Ah, bullshit!

PETER: Look, *Nyoongahs* buy their grog from *Wetjalas*, they break the law and they git jugged by *Wetjalas*. The lawyer's white, the cops are white, the magistrate's white, the warden's white: the whole box and dice is white. Put a *Nyoongah* against all them. I tell you we ain't got a bloody chance.

ELI: Warders, they're no trouble. I know 'ow to handle

them bastards: 'yes sir, no, Warden. I'll do it, sir.' All you gotta do is butter 'em up a bit. Play it smart.

PETER: Playin' along with the system eh?

ROY: Arse lickin' I call it, you're just scareda gettin' belted up.

[ELI *stands up and thumps the table.*]

ELI: Look at this — busted eye, broken nose, busted eardrum, [*pointing to his head*] thirteen stitches! You know who done all that? Not *Wetjalas*, but *Nyoongahs*, me own fuckin' people!

PETER: Man, yer wrong, the system done that to yuh, but yuh can't see it.

ROY: How d'yuh expect him to see it, 'es only got one eye, so 'e reckons.

[*They laugh.* WORRU *pushes his chipped enamel mug across to* PETER.]

WORRU: Come on, boy, gimme *kaep*, gimme *kaep*.

PETER: [*taking the bottle away*] No, Pop, I think you had enough. You know you just come outa hospital.

ELI: Aw, come on. Give the poor ol' fella a drink. One drink won't 'urt 'im. [*Pouring him a drink*] 'Ere y' are, oldy, git that inta yuh.

PETER: Gee, Pop, you look real smart in them new clothes.

[*He picks* WORRU'S *jacket off the floor. His pills fall unnoticed onto the floor.*]

WORRU: Nurse gib 'em to me. She pretty one too.

[*He cackles cheekily.*]

ELI: Yeah. Bet you could tell some stories 'bout you an' them nurses, eh?

WORRU: Yeah! I tell 'em a lotta stories. I tell 'em that one 'bout Cornell an' Milbart, on the train. An' they laugh somethin' cruel. [*Laughing*] Roy! You know that one.

ROY: No, never heard that one, Pop.

WORRU: Yeah, you know.

ELI: No 'e don't, Unc. Come on, what 'appened?

ROY: Yeah, Unc, tell us the yarn.

WORRU: Well, they was gitten old fellas, them two, Cornell and Milbart, they was stayin' in Wagin an' they wanted to git to Katanning Show, see? And they was *wayarning* of the train, real *wayarning*. [*Laughing*] Anyways, they got in a railway carriage and that train was goin' *keert kooliny, keert kooliny* round them bends and them corners. An' — an' — they was . . . they was . . .

[*He coughs and splutters.*]

. . . sitting close together, like.

[*He laughs again and claps his hands.*]

Anyway, they went around one corner and Cornell got a real fright and he shouted '*choo*' and he pushed Milbart like that.

[*He pushes* PETER *almost off his seat.*]

And he said, he said, '*Wart arny yit*, Milbart, git ober in de udder corner an' help me balance this thing before it bloody tips over.'

[*They all laugh,* WORRU *coughs.*]

Ay, boy, give me 'nother drink. 'Urry up, come on!

PETER: Aw right, Pop, but you gotta tell us another yarn now.

WORRU: Aw right, yeah.

[*He stops suddenly.*]

ELI: Yeah, come on, Pop.

WORRU: By rights I shouldn' be tellin' you fellas this. [*Pointing to* ROY] Aw right for 'im.

ROY: It's all right Unc.

WORRU: All right. Well, you know that Christmas tree, that's the *moodgah,* that's the *Nyoongah* name.

PETER: Yeah?

WORRU: Well, when our people was *noych*, their *kunya* — that's what *Wetjala* call soul, *unna*?

ROY: Yeah, that's right, Uncle.

WORRU: Well their *kunya* would go and stay in the *moodgah* tree, some time for a l-o-o-ng time, an' when the *moodgah* flowers were gone, summertime, their *kunya* would leave the *moodgah* an' go to Watjerup. That way, over the sea, Watjerup, thaty way, *boh-oh*.

[*He gestures westward. His audience is mesmerised.*]

PETER: Where's Watjerup, Popeye?

WORRU: *Kia*, Watjerup, that's what *Wetjalas* call Rottnest. An' if you go Mogumber old settlement, lotta *moodgah* up there 'cause, 'cause that be *Nyoongah* country for lo-o-ng time. An' them *moodgah* they strong, they kill other tree if they grow near them, *bantji, muttlegahruk, tjarraly, kudden*, kill 'em, finish, 'cause *kunyas* make him strong an' only *boolya* man can go there near the *moodgah* 'cause the *boolya* man is strong too, like that tree; an' 'e can drink water an' take 'oney from the *moodgah*. Anybody else, that's *warrah*, they could be finish, *unna*?

> [*An eerie silence overcomes them.* PETER *shudders and jumps up.*]

PETER: Come on, this is gettin' too morbid. Let's have some bloody music.

> [*They relax and pour drinks.* PETER *turns the radio on and begins to dance drunkenly.*]

WORRU: [*laughing*] Ah, you don't call that dancin', do you?

ELI: Go on, Pop, git up an' show 'im a real *middar*. Go on, oldy, a real dinkum *yahllarah*.

WORRU: Awright, awright, I'll show you fellas, me an' Nindal we danced for the Prince of New South Wales.

> [WORRU *rises and begins a drunken stumbling version of a half-remembered tribal dance.* PETER *turns the volume up and continues his own disco dance.* WORRU *pushes him aside and dances to the amusement of* ELI *and* ROY, *until his feet tangle and he falls heavily.*
>
> *The scene freezes, the light changes, and the radio cuts abruptly to heavy rhythmic didjiridoo and clap sticks. An intricately painted* DANCER *appears on the escarpment against a dramatic red sky, dances down and across in front of them, pounding his feet into the stage. Finally, he dances back up the ramp where he poses for a moment before the light snaps out on the last note of music.*]

SCENE FIVE

About an hour later. The full bottle is now nearly empty. The heat and the alcohol are taking their toll. WORRU, *now dishevelled, is slumped on the sofa asleep. His handkerchief, shoes and socks lie about the room.* ROY *and* ELI *are half asleep around the table,* PETER *is leaning over the sink gazing blankly through the window. The occasional crow can be heard.*

The stillness is eventually broken by PETER *splashing himself with water.* SHANE *enters, wearily drags his feet across the stage, goes inside and opens the fridge.* MEENA *follows.*

SHANE: Gawd I'm hungry, what's for lunch? [*Spotting* WORRU] Oh hi, Pop, how are you?
MEENA: Hello Pop, you look super. New clothes? You look real *moorditj.*
WORRU: *Kia gnullarah bridaira nyinning.*
    [*They laugh.*]
SHANE: Oh crikey, what's for lunch?
MEENA: You should have got them to shave your beard off.
WORRU: *Yuart! Yuart!*
SHANE: Anything to eat?
MEENA: Where's Mum?
PETER: She's in town, shopping. She'll be back directly.
SHANE: What's the good of that, we'll be back at school by then.
MEENA: And still hungry.
ROY: [*pointing*] Bread there, butter there, some cool drink in the fridge.
    [SHANE *gets a near empty bottle of Coca-Cola from the fridge.* MEENA *tips a stale crust from the bread packet, she butters it, glaring at the wine bottles.*]
MEENA: Why didn't Mum leave us some lunch money?
ELI: [*guiltily*] She's gone to town to get bread and meat.
SHANE: [*emptying his pockets*] I got — ah — nine cents. Anyone build on that? Enough to get a pie.
    [*He tries* ROY, *then* ELI.]

ELI: Aw, we're open.

MEENA: [*picking up the nearly-empty wine bottle*] Looks like it.

> [ELI *points to* UNCLE WORRI *who has dozed off.* SHANE *shuffles across to him and wakes him gently.*]

SHANE: Hey, Popeye, Popeye.

WORRU: [*waking*] Ay, ay, what d'ya want?

SHANE: You got any money to put with this, enough for a pie, Popeye?

WORRU: Ay, what's the matter, boy?

SHANE: I want to get a pie for lunch, I'm hungry.

WORRU: Yeah, here you are.

> [*Coins fall to the floor.* SHANE *swoops on them.*]

SHANE: Oh boy — nine, ten, thirty, forty, fifty, fifty cents. Wow, got enough! Saved from starvation.

MEENA: Sure you got enough?

SHANE: Yeah, enough for one, anyway.

MEENA: Thank you, Popeye Worru, see you later.

SHANE: Thanks Pop, see you!

> [*They sprint out.* MEENA *stops* SHANE *as he runs across the stage, grabbing him by the shirt.*]

MEENA: Half each, remember.

SHANE: Yeah, I know. Come on.

> [*They run off. The men sit in silence.* PETER *wanders across to the table and drops into a chair.* ELI *holds up the nearly-empty bottle and peers into it.* WORRU *dozes off again.*]

ELI: Not much left. Nearly finished.

ROY: Well, if we got none, we go without.

> [ELI *edges across to the sofa and wakes* WORRU.]

ELI: Hey Pop, *boondah wah?*

WORRU: Ay, what?

ELI: You got any *boondah?*

> [WORRU *pretends to sleep.*]

PETER: *Choo kynya*, you got no shame, Eli. Poor old fella.

ELI: Nah, it's all right. I'll give it back to him Thursday night. Pop, you got some *boondah* and I'll go and get another bottle of port for us.

> [WORRU *starts to go through his pockets.*]

Look in this one.

[*He goes to search* WORRU *but* WORRU *pushes him away.*]

WORRU: What do you think I can't see? I got two eyes
not like you, *meowl birt.*

[ELI *laughs.*]

ELI: Oops, sorry Pop.

ROY: Don't worry about him, Uncle, he's got two eyes.

[WORRU *gives* ELI *a handful of change.*]

WORRU: 'Ere. And don't forget bring me some *gnummari.*
You 'ear me?

ELI: Sure, Pop, sure. Now let's see how much we got.
[*Counting*] Bastard.

PETER: What?

ELI: Fifty cents short.

PETER: Hang on, hang on.

[*He goes through his pockets and drops a fifty-cent piece
on the table.*]

ELI: Where did you get that from?

PETER: Aunty Peggy gave it to me for a bus fare.

ROY: I thought you said you came home on the bus this
morning.

PETER: I did! But when the driver asked for my fare I
made out I lost it. He was going to put me off at the
next stop but this old *Wetjala* lady paid my fare.

[ELI *slips the nearly-empty bottle into his pocket, unnoticed
by* ROY *or* WORRU, *pulls his eyepatch over his eye and does
a curious comical shuffle towards the door.*]

ELI: Right, move your black feet, Eli Wallitch, move your
black feet. [*To* PETER] You comin'?

PETER: Yeah, might as well.

ROY: Don't be long. Get back here before the old girl gits
home.

[ELI *and* PETER *step briskly across the stage.* ELI *shows*
PETER *the bottle. They exit quickly laughing.* ROY *empties
his glass and looks about for the bottle, first bewildered
then frantic. He rushes to the door.*]

Eli! Eli! [*Walking back inside*] You fuckin' sly dingo
bastard!

WORRU: Who? Who you *warrah wangeing*?

ROY: Oh that bloody Eli.

WORRU: *Nietjuk?*

ROY: He beats me every fuckin' time.

> [WORRU *dozes off.* ROY *makes a half-hearted attempt to clean up the kitchen, carefully concealing the empty bottle behind the fridge.*]

Hey Pop, Pop.

WORRU: What, what?

ROY: You go lay down for a while.

WORRU: Ay?

ROY: Why don't you have a bit of a rest?

WORRU: *Kia, kia,* I think I will.

> [ROY *helps him to his feet and steers him towards the door.* WORRU *staggers out and flops onto his bed.*]

ROY: Old girl will be home directly and she'll cook us a feed.

> [ROY *sits at the table, puts his feet up and closes his eyes.* WORRU *begins to grunt and mumble incoherently, gradually becoming clearer and building to a shout.*]

WORRU: *Kia* Milbart, Milbart! Where is water, *kaep wah?*

SCENE SIX

Mid afternoon. It is oppressively hot and still. WORRU *is fast asleep sprawled on his bed.* ROY, *also asleep, lolls precariously on a chair with his feet on the table. The slow rhythmic breathing of the sleepers is punctuated by the occasional crow.*

DOLLY, carrying a bulging supermarket bag, trudges wearily across the stage. As she enters the house she stops and surveys the room before creeping in and putting down the groceries. She picks up a mug, sniffs it, rinses it and uses it to drink water. She peers inquisitively about the room, then behind the fridge, where she discovers the wine bottle. Finally, she steals alongside ROY, *gently nudges him off his chair and sits down as he drops limply onto the floor.* ROY *wakes in terror, jumps up and looks around the room.*

ROY: Awgh! What the fuck! Oooh! [*Spotting* DOLLY] Aw,
    'ullo love.
    [*Pause.*]
    'Ow you going?
DOLLY: [*coolly*] I'm all right.
    [*Pause.*]
    Where's the boys?
    [*She begins to unpack the groceries.*]
ROY: What?
DOLLY: Peter an' Eli.
ROY: Oh, they down town somewheres.
DOLLY: Kids been 'ome?
ROY: Yeah, they bin 'ome.
DOLLY: They 'ave lunch, eh?
ROY: Yeah, yeah, yeah.
DOLLY: What they 'ave?
ROY: They 'ad pies an' cool drink.
DOLLY: Didn't you get to the butcher's shop?
ROY: No, they 'ad pies instead.
DOLLY: How's ole fella?
ROY: Oh 'es sleepin, 'es been asleep all mornin'.
    [*She looks about and picks up* UNCLE WORRU's *pills, hand-
    kerchief, shoes and socks.*]
DOLLY: How did these get 'ere?
ROY: Aw, I dunno!
DOLLY: And how'd this get 'ere?
    [*She picks up the empty bottle.*]
    Now where did you git the money from?
ROY: What money?
DOLLY: For this bloody bottle?
ROY: Oh, Eli bought it this morning.
    [*He starts to feel around for his thongs.*]
DOLLY: [*threatening him with the bottle*] Roy Wallitch, you're
    a rotten stinkin' liar. You spent the kids' dinner money
    on this, didn't you?
ROY: I tell you Eli an' Peter got it.
    [*He starts to get up.*]
DOLLY: You're not only useless, you're a bloody liar as

well. You spent the kids' dinner money, didn't you?
Didn't you?

ROY: Shit, I'm gettin' outa 'ere.

DOLLY: You bastard!

[ROY *bolts for the door,* DOLLY *makes to throw the bottle
at him but thinks better of it. She walks across to the table
and drops wearily into a chair.* ROY *hops across the stage
with one thong, stops with a yell, rubs his foot painfully.*]

ROY: Bloody doublegees!

[*He puts his thong on and gallops off.* WORRU, *awoken
by the commotion, rises and stumbles half asleep and half
drunk into the doorway.*]

WORRU: Ay? Ay? Ay? What's goin' on.

DOLLY: Ts, ts, ts! Just look at you, 'ome from the 'ospital
two hours and you're drunk already. 'Ave you taken
your pills?

[*He clumsily feels in his pockets, then shrugs his shoulders.*]

WORRU: Must be there somewheres.

[*She picks them up off the table and gets a glass of water.
He walks across and sits down, doing his best to appear
sober.*]

DOLLY: I dunno what I'm gonna do with you, looks like
you wanna die, eh?

WORRU: Aw, leave me alone.

DOLLY: You'll be all alone down in the cemetery.

WORRU: I don't care, you can chuck me on th' ant 'eap
if you wanna.

DOLLY: [*giving him the pills*] Come on, take these.

[*He refuses.*]

Or would you sooner go an' 'ave a needle in the hospital, eh?

[*He takes them.*]

You wanna cuppa tea? Ay Uncle, wanna *marngk*?

WORRU: *Kia.*

[*He wipes his nose with his hand.* DOLLY *gets his handkerchief and catches him just before he blows his nose bush
fashion on the floor.*]

DOLLY: Ah, don't do that.

[*She attempts to wipe his nose but he snatches the hand-*

kerchief and pushes her away. She goes to the sink and begins to make a cup of tea.]

WORRU: Ay, where did that fella go?

DOLLY: What fella?

WORRU: You know, Milbart, 'e come 'ere.

DOLLY: When did 'e come here?

WORRU: Dinnertime.

DOLLY: Oh, Uncle Worru, he's been dead *koora, kwotjut noych*, he died Moore River.

WORRU: *Yuart*, 'e come 'ere talkin' to 'im in there.

DOLLY: It's all in your mind, Uncle, an' that's because you been drinkin' again.

[*She makes the tea,* WORRU *shakes his head as if trying to clear his mind.*]

I remember that old man. Us kids used to go out robbin' beehives with him.

WORRU: Yeah! Yeah! [*Laughing*] I remember bee stung you on the *tjenna* once, down Kunjaberrin swamp, an' I 'ad to carry you 'ome on me *moorlin*, nearly six mile. You was real *tjuelara* bony fella, but you was cruel 'eavy for little *yorga*.

DOLLY: Yeah. [*Laughing*] Ay, Unc? Uncle Worru? You remember Billy Kimberley?

WORRU: Ole Billy Kimberley, *kia*, not young Billy; that old man was *moorditj* with a *kylie*. He could make it go three times 'round that football ground and come back right near his *tjenna*. An' he used to ride that 'orse, 'member: Black — Black 'abit. [*Clapping his hands and laughing*] An' when 'e used to ride that 'orse you couldn't see him at night 'cause 'e was black and the 'orse was black. Proper *moornawooling*, them two. *Kia*. [*Laughing*] An' when 'e used to ride up the river the kids used to hide in the bushes and call out '*Wahrdung* . . . *Wahrdung* . . . Black Crow . . . Black Crow . . .' an' he used to allus carry a long *gidtji*, nor'-west one, an' he would ride over to them boys and yell out, 'Which boy call me black crow, which boy call me black crow?' And them boys would laugh and *doogeearkiny* down the river.

[*They laugh.*]
Yeah, but 'e was bad man, Billy Kimberley. Some of
them trackers was real *warrah*, you know when them
yorgas was sent to work for *wetjalas*. [*Miming a pregnant
woman*] And sometimes they would come back *bootjari*,
and when them *koolangarahs* was born, them trackers,
Billy Kimberley and Bluey too, [*miming choking*] they
would *woort beerny* them babies an' bury them in the
pine plantation, night time.

DOLLY: Oh, no Uncle Worru, is that true?

WORRU: *Kia kunarn, kunarn!*

DOLLY: What 'appened to them fellas?

WORRU: The *kwotjut nyoch*, finish. Yeah, lotta fellas finish
there, Mogumber, Dulung, Binyl, Marrio, Jigalong,
Winarn. You remember Winarn, ol' fella with *doot*
arm? [*Chuckling*] Yeah, yeah, he pinched a bottle a
whisky from his boss an' he got cruel drunk 'an 'e
rolled in the fire and burnt his arm right off —
[*pointing*] this one, no, no, that one.

DOLLY: [*laughing*] U-n-c-l-e!

[SHANE, MEENA *and their* Wetjala *friend* DARREN *enter
and sprint across the stage outside the house playing keeping-off with a basketball.*]

WORRU: Warrah Place, Mogumber, awright daytime, but
gnank weerdiny, couldn't walk around, stay near the
fire. [*Shuddering*] Too many *tjennuks, moorlies*, an', an'
widartjies. [*Gesturing north*] They come from that way.
They was real bad. Round face, an' they was white,
jus' like *Wetjalas*, an' they 'ad red eyes, an' red 'air, an'
them scream, an' shout, sing out in the night time, in
the pine plantation, jus' like *koolongahs*.

[SHANE *pushes* DARREN *through the door and throws the
ball to him.* DARREN *falls and yells as he catches it.* WORRU
and DOLLY *get an enormous fright.*]
Allewah!

DOLLY: *Choo*! *Choo*! You frightened the livin' daylights
out of me.

DARREN: Sorry.

[SHANE *and* MEENA *enter.*]

SHANE: [*laughing*] Sorry, Mum.

DOLLY: What are you chuckin' the ball around the house for?

SHANE: We was just playing keepings off Meena.

DARREN: I'm sorry, Mrs Wallitch.

DOLLY: It's all right.

MEENA: Did you get a fright, Popeye?

WORRU: *Kia*, thought he was bloody *widartji*.

MEENA: Chuck it here.

SHANE: Hey Mum? Anythin' to eat, I'm starvin'.

MEENA: Me too.

DOLLY: Bread and butter and some Vegemite there.
  [MEENA *begins to butter slices of bread.*]

SHANE: [*pushing in*] Hurry up. Gawd you're slow.

MEENA: Aw, just wait. You're not the only one that's hungry.

WORRU: [*to* DARREN] Ay, boy.

DOLLY: And spread some for Darren too, Shane.

WORRU: Ay, ay, boy.

SHANE: I will, soon as she gives me the knife.

WORRU: Ay, ay, boy.
  [*He beckons to* DARREN *who walks gingerly up to him.*]
  You *Wetjala* or *Nyoongah*?

DARREN: What?

SHANE: Hey, Popeye, he's a *Wetjala*.

MEENA: You don't see *Nyoongahs* with red hair, Popeye.
  [*They laugh.* SHANE *and* MEENA *eat ravenously.*]

DOLLY: Didn't you kids have lunch?

SHANE: Aw, yeah.

DOLLY: What did you have?

SHANE: We had a pie.

MEENA: Yeah, and he ate three-quarters of it. Eh, Mum, they were all drinking here at lunchime. [*Pointing to* WORRU] Him too.
  [WORRU *pretends to sleep.* DARREN *moves closer and stares at him.*]

DOLLY: Yeah, I know, I know.

SHANE: Where's Dad?

DOLLY: [*laughing wryly*] He went out that door.

[DARREN *continues to stare at* UNCLE WORRU *from close range.* WORRU *suddenly roars and makes an ineffectual grab at him.* DARREN *gets a fright and jumps behind* SHANE *for protection.*]

SHANE: Let go, he's all right, he won't hurt you.

MEENA: [*laughing*] Oh, Popeye.

DOLLY: Uncle Worru, don't scare him like that.

WORRU: [*beckoning to* DARREN] Ay boy. Come 'ere, *wetjala*, come 'ere.

SHANE: [*pushing him*] Go on, go on, he won't hurt you, go on, talk to him.

WORRU: Ay. [*Pointing to his beard*] Do you know what this is, *Nyoongah* way? This is my *gnarnuk*. [*Pointing to his nose*] This my *moorly*. [*Pointing to his eye*] And this my *meow*. [*Indicating his forehead*] And this my *yimmung*. [*Cackling with delight*] Plenty *nyoondiak* there, *kia*, plenty *nyoondiak*.

[MEENA *picks up the ball.*]

DOLLY: [*beginning to prepare supper*] Oh, I forgot to get tomatoes. Meena, Meena!

MEENA: [*bouncing the ball*] Yes, Mother.

DOLLY: Will you go down an' get me some tomatoes?

MEENA: OK.

DOLLY: [*giving her some money*] Here. Get me a kilo.

SHANE: We'll come with you. Can we get a bottle of cool drink?

DOLLY: I s'pose, an' don't be long.

SHANE: Thanks, Mum. [*To* DARREN] Come on.

[*The children appear at the front bouncing the ball.* SHANE *intercepts the ball and throws it to* DARREN. *The following conversation is punctuated by a game of keeping-off. Inside,* DOLLY *makes damper.*]

DARREN: Hey, that old man, is he for real?

SHANE: He sure is.

DARREN: How old is he?

SHANE: Must be nearly a hundred.

MEENA: Nah, no he's not, he's about eighty.

DARREN: What language did he talk?

MEENA: Oh that's just *Nyoongah* talk.

DARREN: Can you talk it?

SHANE: Nah, not really.

DARREN: What did he mean by noon . . . noon . . .

MEENA: *Nyoondiak?* That means brains.

DARREN: What was for eye?

[MEENA *and* SHANE *look at each other blankly.*]

MEENA: I dunno.

[*She giggles.*]

SHANE: Don't ask me, I wouldn't have a clue. I know what *Wetjala* is, that's you!

[MEENA *grabs the ball and runs.*]

MEENA: Come on you two, Mum said hurry.

[*They exit.*]

WORRU: [*cackling with glee*] That *Wetjala nop* got a cruel fright.

DOLLY: [*kneading the damper*] That wasn't nice, Uncle Worru.

WORRU: Ain't he ever seen a *Nyoongah* before?

DOLLY: *Nyoornditj*, he's a *winyarn*.

[WORRU *laughs dismissively.*]

Wasn't you ever frightened, when you was little?

WORRU: *Kia.* Plenty times and I know you used to be when you was a little fella at Mogumber. You *koolongarah* used to sleep together like puppy dawgs all covered with blankets from head to foots, even 'ot nights.

DOLLY: Yeah, I remember.

WORRU: Good place summertime, *moorditj*, plenty *dytje*, honey, berries and them *kohn*, big like that, taste like 'taters.

DOLLY: And them summer beetles, [*holding her thumb and forefinger about five centimetres apart*] they used to be that long and us girls used to get a piece of cotton from the sleeves of our dresses and tie notes on their legs and throw the beetle up in the air and they would fly away and we wished some boy would find them and read the notes. [*Laughing*] That's how I met Roy. I don't know whether to be thankful for that beetle or not.

[*They fall silent.* DOLLY *puts her hand on* WORRU's *arm.* PETER *enters and saunters across the stage outside the house carrying a leg of kangaroo.*]
And you know that was the last time I saw a corroboree at Moore River.

WORRU: [*excitedly*] *Kia, kia,* the *yongarah* dance, the *waitj* dance, the *karda,* the *yahllarah,* the *middar,* the *nyumby,* the *nyumby . . .* the *nyumby. Yuart,* they all finish now, all gone.

DOLLY: Never mind, Uncle, you're still with us, you're *moorditj,* you gonna live to be one hundred.

PETER: [*bursting in*] Hi, look what I got.

DOLLY: Where d'you get that from?

WORRU: *Yonga, woolah!*

PETER: Got it from Aunty Peg.

DOLLY: That'll come in handy.

WORRU: You gotta bacon cook with that?

DOLLY: I'll get some, Unc. [*Feeling the roo*] My, young one too, nice and tender. Now Peter, I want you to go down and phone up my request.

PETER: Right, who's it to?

DOLLY: To Auntie Rose and the boys at Gnowangerup.

PETER: Reggy and Zac still in gaol, Mum.

DOLLY: I thought they done their time.

PETER: Nah, Zac got moved to Pardellup and Reggy was out on parole but he broke it and now he's back in again.

DOLLY: You write it out, you know how to do it.

PETER: [*writing on his arm*] From Dolly, Roy, Peter . . .

DOLLY: Better put Eli in.

PETER: . . . Eli, Shane and Meena Wallitch.

DOLLY: And Uncle Worru.

PETER: . . . and Uncle Worru. [*Reading*] To Auntie Rose and the boys at Gnowangerup and Reggy at Wooroloo and Zac at Pardellup. Hey, what song?

DOLLY: 'Me and Bobby McGee', Charlie Pride. Now go down and ring up straight away, and bring some bacon back and don't mess around now 'cause I need that bacon for supper.

[*She gives him some money. He walks to the door.*]
And make sure you read it out nice and clear over
the phone.

PETER: Yeah, OK.

[PETER *walks across the stage counting the money and
exits.* WORRU *stands up and stretches.*]

WORRU: I think I go *bitjarra gnoorndiny* for a little while.

DOLLY: Yes, Unc, you go and have a rest. I'll wake you
up supper time.

[WORRU *wanders into his bedroom and lies down.* DOLLY
*dusts the damper, places it in the oven and washes her
hands.* WORRU *mumbles to himself, gradually becoming
louder and more coherent.*]

WORRU: Milbart, Milbart, Milbart! *Gidjti wah*, Milbart.
Make a spear, I wanna catch a *kulkana*. Make spear,
Milbart! *Gidjti wah!*

[*Didjeridoo crashes in, the lights change. The* DANCER
*appears at front of stage and in stylised rhythmic steps
searches for a straight stick, finds it, straightens it, pares
and tips it before sprinting up the ramp onto the escarpment
and striking the* mirrolgah *stance against a dramatic
sunset as the music climaxes and cuts.*]

SCENE SEVEN

Dusk, still hot. Cicadas drone in the background. WORRU *is
asleep in his bed. A pot of kangaroo stew simmers on the stove.*
MEENA *sits on the sofa completing an elaborate project.* SHANE
is sprawled on the floor struggling with geography homework.
DOLLY *is sweeping.*

She pushes SHANE *aside, sweeps under him and continues
on.*

SHANE: Meena! Hey, Meena?

MEENA: What?

SHANE: What's the capital of Wales?

MEENA: [*absorbed in her own homework*] Cardiff.

SHANE: What?

MEENA: Card-iff.

> [SHANE *writes carefully.*]

DOLLY: Meena, Meena?

MEENA: [*sighing*] Yes, Mum.

DOLLY: Get a bit of newspaper.

MEENA: OK.

> [*She reluctantly gets some newspaper and uses it as a pan for her mother to sweep the dirt into.*]

SHANE: What's the capital of London? Meena! What's the capital of London?

MEENA: Aw Mum, he's gotta be joking.

DOLLY: Why?

MEENA: Didn't you hear what he said? How dumb can you get?

SHANE: OK, I just asked a question.

MEENA: Now listen, Shane, London is the capital city of England.

SHANE: Oh.

> [*Pause.*]

Where's Eden-berg?

MEENA: Where?

SHANE: Eden-berg.

MEENA: I dunno, give us a look.

SHANE: See. You don't know everything.

MEENA: Edinburgh, stupid — the capital of Scotland and Ireland. The country is spelt I-R-E-L-A-N-D, not I-S-L-A-N-D.

SHANE: [*resentfully*] I dunno.

> [*He throws the homework book down, unfolds a comic and begins reading.*]

DOLLY: Meena, take that rubbish out and put it in the bin. Come on, there's enough flies in here already.

MEENA: Aw, Mum, make Shane do it. I gotta finish a ten-page assignment on Aborigines tomorrow.

> [ROY *enters, slightly drunk, and walks across the stage outside the house.*]

DOLLY: All right Shane. Come on, Shane!

SHANE: All right.

> [*He takes it out, still reading his comic.*]

Dad's coming!

> [ROY *enters the house sheepishly.* DOLLY *ignores him. He walks across to the stove.*]

ROY: Eh, I can smell 'roo. Where did you get that from?

DOLLY: Sister Peg give it to me.

ROY: What? No bacon?

DOLLY: No. I sent Peter down for some two hours ago. Did you see him down there anywhere?

ROY: No.

DOLLY: What about goin' down see if you can see where he is.

ROY: Ah, he'll be all right, stop fussin', woman.

DOLLY: All right.

ROY: Anyway, he's most likely with Eli.

DOLLY: Forget about the bloody bacon then.

MEENA: Eh, Pop?

ROY: Yeah.

MEENA: I just worked out something amazing: you know how Aborigines have been in Australia for at least forty thousand years, right?

ROY: So they reckon.

MEENA: And if there was three hundred thousand here when Captain Cook came, that means that . . . that . . . hm, hang on, hang on . . .

SHANE: Come on, what's the big news then?

MEENA: Shut up you . . . listen . . . forty thousand years plus, three hundred thousand people, that means that over twelve million Aborigines have lived and died in Australia before the white man came.

ROY: Dinkum?

SHANE: Oh boy, they must've shot a lotta 'roos and ate a lotta dampers.

MEENA: They didn't shoot them.

SHANE: I know! Three dampers a day for forty thousand years, how many's that, Pop?

ROY: I dunno, better ask your mother.

DOLLY: Me, I wouldn't have a clue.

MEENA: You don't count it up like that, slowly. Anyway, flour is white man's food. Aborigines used grass seeds. [*Reading from a book*] Jam seeds, wattle seeds, and—

DOLLY: [*removing the damper from the oven*] OK. Who wants a feed instead of just talkin' about it?

SHANE: [*jumping up*] Me!
[*He sprints to the table.* DOLLY *intercepts him.*]

DOLLY: Go and ask the old bloke if he's getting up for supper.
[SHANE *goes out to* WORRU's *bed and attempts to wake him.* DOLLY *and* MEENA *serve the stew.* ROY *breaks up the damper.*]

ROY: [*sniffing his stew*] Wonder where that boy got to?

SHANE: Popeye?

DOLLY: You said not to worry about him.

SHANE: Popeye?

DOLLY: Remember?

SHANE: Ay, Popeye!

ROY: How much money did you give him?

DOLLY: Two dollars.

SHANE: You getting up for supper, or you wanta eat it in here?

WORRU: What?

ROY: Bet he met up with that bloody Eli and they're down at the Exchange.

SHANE: You getting up for supper, Pop?

WORRU: *Kia.*

DOLLY: Just listen who's talkin'.
[SHANE *helps* WORRU *into the kitchen.*]

SHANE: We got 'roo and damper for supper, Pop.
[ROY *starts to eat.*]

WORRU: *Woolah, yongah, kwobinyarn, kwobinyarn.*

DOLLY: Roy, you say grace.

SHANE: Do we only say grace when we are eating kangaroo?

ROY: [*putting his spoon back on his plate and swallowing*] We thank you, Lord, for what —

WORRU: You put some bacon in this?

ROY: We thank you —

WORRU: Bacon, *wah*?

SHANE: Ssh, ssh, Popeye, close your eyes.

ROY: We thank you, Lord.

WORRU: What for? Can't eat with me eyes closed.

ROY: We thank you, Lord, for what we have got.

WORRU: [*to* SHANE, *pointing upwards*] I forgot about that
   fella up there.

ROY: Oh, Gawd!

WORRU: *Choo, kynya*, shame, eh?

   [*They all laugh, except* ROY *who tries again.*]

ROY: [*yelling*] All right, shut up! [*Guiltily*] We thank you,
   Lord, for what we got for . . . your sake an' ours too.

DOLLY: Amen.

WORRU: *Kia*.

   [*They eat in silence.* DOLLY *suddenly jumps up and turns
   the radio on. It is the Earl Reeve 6WF Tuesday Night
   Country Music Request Programme: Jimmy Little singing
   'Baby Blue'.*]

   Winjar mahngk?

DOLLY: Meena, fill this mug up for him.

   [*They eat.* MEENA *pours* WORRU's *tea.*]

MEENA: Popeye, why do *Nyoongahs* call that one *mahngk*?

WORRU: Eh?

MEENA: That one Popeye. Why do *Nyoongahs* call it *mahngk*?

WORRU: That's his name. You see leaf on a tree, that's
   a *mahngk*, that one *mahngk* too, tea leaf.

   [ELI *enters wearing an eyepatch and strides across the
   stage outside the house, carrying a flagon of port.*]

MEENA: That's gotta go in my project.

   [*She scribbles in her pad. They return to hearty eating.*
   ELI *enters, sighs and sits at the table.*]

ROY: Where's d'you come from?

DOLLY: Did you see Peter?

ELI: The Exchange.

   [DOLLY *places a meal in front of him.*]

ROY: What'd I tell you?

DOLLY: Did you see Peter?

ELI: Yeah.

ROY: Where's the bacon?

ELI: What fuckin' bacon?

DOLLY: Where is he?

ELI: I think he's up at the police station.

ROY: What?

DOLLY: What for?

ELI: I dunno, he was in a car with a mob of young blokes. Anyway *manatj* pulled 'em up and bunged 'em all in the rat van.

ROY: Where was you?

ELI: They never seen me, I kept outa the road.

ROY: Yeah, trust you.

ELI: What did you expect me to do? You know them bastards don't like me.

ROY: I don't blame 'em.

DOLLY: All right, that's enough, come on.

MEENA: Was probably a stolen car, Mum.

DOLLY: I know.

> [ROY *prepares to pour himself a drink.*]

You put that down, you're comin' with me.

ROY: Aw, you and Meena go, love. What can I do? You know I can't talk.

DOLLY: You get on your bloody black feet and walk right out that door.

ROY: All right!

> [*They leave.* MEENA *leaves the table and continues with her homework.* ELI *pours two mugs of port.*]

WORRU: Where they goin'?

ELI: Aw, they just gone to see where Peter is. They be back drecktly.

> [ROY *reluctantly follows* DOLLY *across the stage.*]

ROY: A night in the lock-up would do him good.

ELI: 'Ere, get this into you, Unc.

DOLLY: No son of mine is goin' to gaol, not if I can help it.

[DOLLY *and* ROY *exit.*]

WORRU: *Kia, kia.*

ELI: [*Pointing to his eyepatch*] Yeah, me and old patchy had a good day, Pop.

[*He takes it off and puts it in his pocket.*]

WORRU: Patchy?

ELI: Yeah, we were doin' all right outside the shopping centre today, yeah, gettin' fifty cents a bite. One *wetjala* bloke, hippy, he give me two dollars.

WORRU: *Kia*, two dollar.

ELI: Anyways, some of them *Nyoongahs* spotted me. There they was: 'Give me fifty cents, brother', 'Give me a dollar, nephew', 'Give me fifty cents, uncle'; and you know none of them black bastards are related to me. That's true. Pop, I never seen blackfellas like 'em, they real bloody dinkum out and out bludgers. Can't stand the bastards.

[WORRU *knocks back his port and pours another.* ELI *turns the radio to full volume.* MEENA *looks up from her homework.*]

MEENA: Do you have to have it that loud?

ELI: That's a solid song. Jimmy Little . . . 'Baby Blue'.

[ELI *sings along drunkenly and pretends to play a guitar.*]

MEENA: Wouldn't want to be in your shoes when Mum comes home.

[*She storms out with her project and gets up on* WORRU's *bed.*]

ELI: [*laughing stupidly*] I take 'em off, then.

[*He flings his shoes about the room and settles down with* WORRU *to an evening's drinking as Earl Reeve announces* DOLLY's *request. 'Me and Bobby McGee' fades with the lights.*

Clap sticks are heard and the DANCER *appears sitting cross-legged on the escarpment against a deep night sky. He sings, accompanying himself with the clap sticks.*]

DANCER:
>   *Wahra biny, wahra biny,*
>   *Koor Ndillah boorndilly doniny.*
>   *Yoongoo bootjahrahk kippulyiny kippulyiny,*
>   *Mahri wahrabiny, wahrabiny, wahrabiny,*
>   *Woolah!*
>
>   ['Look at the clouds rolling, rolling,
>   Thunder crashing, smashing.
>   The rain has soaked the earth.
>   Clouds rolling, rolling, rolling,
>   Hoorah!']
> [*The lights snap out on the final beat.*]

SCENE EIGHT

It is 12.15 am. The radio is crackling. SHANE *is asleep on the sofa,* ELI *is stretched out snoring on the floor.* MEENA *is asleep in* UNCLE WORRU'S *room.* UNCLE WORRU *is attempting the overwhelmingly difficult task of pouring himself a mug of port from the flagon. He seems to spend hours trying to direct a few splashes into his mug. He eventually drops the mug on the floor.*

   DOLLY, ROY *and* PETER *enter, walk wearily across the stage and go inside. They stand just inside the door and survey the devastation.*

DOLLY: Oh, no . . .
>   [WORRU *greets them with a clumsy gesture and an un-intelligible grunt.* ROY *turns the radio off.* WORRU *babbles incoherently.*]
>   [*to* PETER, *pointing to* SHANE] Wake him up. Put him to bed.
PETER: Eh, Shane . . . Come on, wake up, brother.
SHANE: Uh . . . uh . . . uh.
PETER: Come to bed, come on.
>   [*He guides* SHANE *off.*]
SHANE: What happened to you?

PETER: Aw nothin', I'm awright.

[DOLLY *starts to clean up the mess.* WORRU *babbles on.*
DOLLY *goes out to* WORRU's *room and attempts to wake*
MEENA. PETER *returns.*]

ROY: [*to* PETER] Gimme a lift with the old bloke.

DOLLY: Meena. Come on, Meena.

ROY: Come on young fella, *tjen kooliny.*

DOLLY: Wake up, Meena.

ROY: *Gnoorndiny* for you.

MEENA: Aw, aw, what's happened?

DOLLY: Nothing, come on.

[MEENA *sleepily follows* DOLLY *into the kitchen.* ROY *and*
PETER *eventually drag* WORRU, *who is paralytic and unco-*
operative, to his feet and attempt to direct him towards the
door.]

ROY: Gawd the old bugger's heavy.

WORRU: [*yelling*] Ay, ay, *winjar koorl*, where we goin'?
Gnuny nooniny barminy.

[*He thrashes about and elbows* ROY *in the stomach.* ROY
folds up.]

Ay, leave me alone, *gnuny nooniny bahkininy.*

[WORRU *bites* PETER *viciously on the forearm,* ROY *grabs*
WORRU *who is about to topple.*]

PETER: Oh, geez, he bit me.

ROY: Come on Peter, give us a hand. Come on, Popeye,
what's the matter with you.

[*They eventually get him, struggling all the way, through*
the door and dump him on his bed. MEENA's *homework*
is trampled underfoot; ROY *attempts to gather it up and*
returns to the kitchen with PETER. DOLLY *throws a blanket*
over ELI.]

WORRU: Fuckin' bastards.

MEENA: [*to* ROY] What happened?

ROY: Ask him.

MEENA: [*trying to put her homework back in order*] Well?

PETER: Got picked up for ridin' in a stolen car.

MEENA: What did you get in it for?

PETER: Aw, I didn't know it was stolen. Anyway, they

said they would drive me home, and I just got in the
car when wheek! — the cops pulled us up.

MEENA: What time is it?

DOLLY: It's about half past twelve.

MEENA: Aw, gawd. I'm goin' to bed. Good night,
everybody.

[*She goes.*]

PETER: Me too.

[*He begins to walk off, stops, takes a packet of bacon out
of his pocket and drops it on the table.*]

Mum, Dad, thanks for gettin' me out.

[ROY *raises a clenched fist.* PETER *exits.* ROY *looks at*
DOLLY, *points to the flagon then to* DOLLY. *She nods.* ROY
*pours the last of the port into a mug. The lights fade as
he passes it to* DOLLY. *She drinks and passes it to* ROY.
Blackout.]

SCENE NINE

A narrow beam of light reveals WORRU *alone downstage.*

WORRU:

You have turned our land into a desolate
place.
We stumble along with a half white mind.
Where are we?
What are we?
Not a recognised race.
There is a desert ahead and a desert
behind.

[*The soft distant sound of children singing a tribal song
is heard. The tribal family of Scene One walk slowly back
across the escarpment against a night sky. They are in
chains.*]

The tribes are all gone,
The boundaries are broken;
Once we had bread here,
You gave us stone.

We are tired of the benches,
Our beds in the park;
We welcome the sundown
That heralds the dark.
White lady methylate
Keep us warm and from crying,
Hold back the hate
And hasten the dying.

The tribes are all gone,
The spears are all broken;
Once we had bread here
You gave us stone.

[*The light on* WORRU *fades out. The singing becomes
louder as the family disappears and the sky fades to black
as the song finishes.*]

ACT TWO

MOORGA — WINTER

SCENE ONE

A cold wet winter afternoon.

The kitchen/living room is shabby and untidy, dirty dishes piled up on the sink, rubbish, bottles, cigarette packets on the floor. Clean clothes are draped over a chair in front of a single bar radiator. WORRU's *bed has been turned around, his room is squalid.*

An eerie traditional chant as the family of Scenes One and Ten trudge across the escarpment against a bleak, wintry sky. The women lead carrying an assortment of boxes and bundles. They are inadequately dressed in blankets and shabby period clothes.

As the sound fades and they disappear, a light builds on WORRU *lying on his bed moaning and mumbling a mournful litany, half English, half* Nyoongah. *He coughs painfully, raises himself and staggers feebly into the kitchen.*

WORRU: Ay! Ay! Dolly. *Winjar? Winjar noonuk?* Aw, aw, aw, Shane! Shane! Where that *nop?* Shane? Shane?
    [*He flops into a chair, exhausted.*]
    Dolly, Dolly.
    [MEENA *enters and walks briskly across the stage outside the house carrying a school bag.* SHANE *follows, occasionally kicking her bag deliberately to annoy her.* WORRU *lifts himself up and staggers across to the sink and attempts to get a mug of water. He fails, staggers back to his chair, falls into it and collapses limply onto the table.* SHANE *and* MEENA *enter the house noisily.*]
SHANE: Hi, everybody!
    [*He stops in his tracks when he sees* WORRU.]
    Meena!

[*They run across to him and try to wake him.*]

Popeye, Popeye! It's me, Shane. You all right, Popeye?

[WORRU *groans.*]

Oh, what did they have to leave him on his own for?

MEENA. Push him back, steady, steady.

SHANE: Come on, Popeye.

MEENA: How are you? You feel all right?

[WORRU *groans.*]

You sick, Popeye?

[WORRU *grunts.*]

Shane, go and get a wet towel, quick!

[*He panics and runs the other way to the sink.*]

Hurry, Shane!

SHANE: All right, don't panic.

[*They mop* WORRU'S *face and sit him up straight. He responds.*]

WORRU: Where's your mother?

SHANE: She's comin' back today.

WORRU: Where'd she go?

MEENA: She went up to Woorooloo, to see Peter.

WORRU: Where *baal koorliny*?

MEENA: What, Popeye?

SHANE: She's stayin' in Northam at Auntie — what's her name?

MEENA: Auntie Elaine.

WORRU: Who?

SHANE: Auntie Elaine!

MEENA: Never mind, he wouldn't know.

WORRU: [*angrily*] 'Course I know, she got one of the Stacks, old Harold's boy, Alfie.

MEENA: Popeye, you want a drink of tea?

WORRU: Ay?

MEENA: Want a *mahngk*?

WORRU: No . . . give me water.

[*She goes to the sink.*]

I'm *minditj, koong minditj.*

[*He rubs his side.* MEENA *puts the cup to his lips, he drinks then coughs violently and splutters water everywhere.*]

MEENA: I think we'd better put him back in bed, get him by the arm. We gonna take you back to your bed, Popeye.

[*He resists, pushing her away.*]

You tell him, he'll get up for you.

SHANE: [*putting his arms around* WORRU] Come on, Popeye. We want you to go and lay down. Then we make you nice big cup of tea.

WORRU: [*painfully getting up*] All right.

[SHANE *guides and struggles with him to the door.*]

SHANE I'll take him, you put the pot on.

[*They stumble through the doorway.*]

MEENA: Watch out he don't fall.

SHANE: It's all right. [*Putting him to bed*] Here, wait on, I'll fix your pillow for you.

[SHANE *covers him.* WORRU *pushes the blanket off.*]

Don't chuck the blanket off, Popeye!

WORRU: It's too 'ot. *Karlawoorliny.*

[SHANE *patiently puts the blankets over him again.*]

SHANE: S'not, it's cold.

[SHANE *enters the main room shaking his arms.*]

Phew, he's heavy. I'm getting ready for footy practice.

[*He exits.*]

MEENA: Plenty of time, we can't go anywhere till they get home.

SHANE: [*off*] Did you wash my footy shorts?

MEENA: Yeah.

SHANE: [*entering*] Where are they?

MEENA: Here!

[*She gets them off the chair in front of the radiator and throws them to him.*]

Here!

SHANE: [*feeling them*] They're wet!

[*He holds them in front of the radiator.* MEENA *folds and re-arranges her clothes.*]

MEENA: Geez, so are these.

SHANE: What, are you going out tonight?

MEENA: Yeah, later maybe.

SHANE: With your boyfriend?

MEENA: I haven't got a boyfriend.

SHANE: What about Ross Mumblin?

MEENA: What about him?

SHANE: You've been out with him every night since Mum's been away.

MEENA: So what?

SHANE: You wanna watch it.

MEENA: Why?

SHANE: He might be a relation, you know we got hundreds of 'em.

MEENA: Nah, his lot come from Wyndham, somewhere up there.

SHANE: [*laughing*] Yeah, he'd have to with a name like that.

[*The noise of a car is heard in the distance.* SHANE *lacing his football boots*] Is that his car?

MEENA: Yeah.

SHANE: Has he got a licence?

MEENA: I dunno, s'pose he has.

SHANE: Thought you had basketball practice tonight.

MEENA: Nah, not going.

SHANE: You better stop home tonight. I think Popeye's pretty sick.

MEENA: Yeah, I know.

SHANE: You better wait until they get home.

MEENA: They'll be drunk, anyway.

SHANE: Yeah, Social Service cheques today.

[*A car pulls up outside, doors slam.* SHANE *runs across to the sink and peers out.*]

Hey, might be Mum.

[DOLLY *and her nephew,* ROBERT, *enter and walk across the stage.* ROBERT *carries a suitcase, he is in his mid-twenties and smartly dressed.*]

MEENA: Nah, too early, bus don't get in till six o'clock.

SHANE: Nah, it's Mum, it is, she must have got a lift with someone.

MEENA: Who?

SHANE: I dunno.

MEENA: Probably Uncle Alf.

SHANE: No . . . it's a young guy. Hi!

[DOLLY *and* ROBERT *enter the house.*]

MEENA: Hi, am I glad you're home.

DOLLY: [*laughing*] Hullo, hullo. Shane, Meena, you know who this is, your cousin Robert, Aunty Elaine's eldest boy. He drove me home.

ROBERT: [*shaking hands with* SHANE] Hi. [*Shaking hands with* MEENA] Hi.

DOLLY: You should remember him, he was stayin' with us when we was at Grass Valley.

MEENA: Yeah, ah, I think so.

ROBERT: Oh yeah, I remember you all right, you were the one that stuck your big toe in the bobtail's mouth.

MEENA: [*embarrassed*] Oh, yeah.

DOLLY: [*laughing*] You went round and round with that *yuron* stuck to your toe.

ROBERT: Think that poor old bobby got more of a fright than you did.

SHANE: Hey Mum, did you see Peter?

DOLLY: Yeah . . . he's all right . . . he's gettin' fat. How's Popeye Worru?

[*Silence.*]

Is he all right?

SHANE: He's been sick, Mum.

DOLLY: Where is he?

SHANE: He's out the back in bed.

MEENA: He's got a pain in his side. [*Demonstrating*] Round here. I was just making him a drink of tea.

[*She makes the tea.*]

DOLLY: Better see how he is.

SHANE: Aw, he's probably asleep, Mum, we've just got him to bed.

[DOLLY *goes out to* WORRU's *room.*]

ROBERT: What, you got footy practice?

SHANE: Yeah.

ROBERT: Who do ya play for?

SHANE: Aw, South Midland, under fourteens, but I barrack for Swan Districts. Narkle brothers, they're solid, eh?

ROBERT: Yeah, solid.

[DOLLY *returns.*]

DOLLY: He's sleeping. Has he been taking his medicine and his pills?

MEENA: Yeah, Shane gives it to him, he won't take it from anybody else.

SHANE: What's the time?

ROBERT: Four forty-eight.

SHANE: Geez, coach'll murder me.

[*He picks up his wet shorts.*]

ROBERT: Where you got to go?

SHANE: Bassendean.

ROBERT: I'll run you there.

SHANE: Will you? Oh boy . . . hang on while I get my gear.

ROBERT: I'll drop into Auntie Peg's and bring him back later.

[SHANE *sprints out.*]

SHANE: See you.

ROBERT: See you later, Auntie Bobtail.

DOLLY: See youse later.

[SHANE *and* ROBERT *leave and jog across the front of the stage.* MEENA *re-arranges her clothes in front of the radiator.*]

SHANE: Do you play footy?

ROBERT: Yeah.

SHANE: Who for?

ROBERT: Railways.

SHANE: What position?

ROBERT: Rover, usually.

[*They exit.* DOLLY *sits down.* MEENA *wipes up at the sink.*]

DOLLY: What about that cuppa tea?

[MEENA *pours two mugs of tea.*]

MEENA: Mum, Robert's solid, eh?

DOLLY: Yeah, he's a nice boy; smart, and he's got a good job.

MEENA: What's he do?

DOLLY: He's a legal aid officer. He's seeing someone in

Perth while he's here and he's gonna try and get Peter out on work release.

[MEENA *checks and re-arranges her clothes again.*]

I thought you had basketball practice Thursday nights?

MEENA: I have, but I told them I wouldn't be there tonight.

DOLLY: Why?

MEENA: I don't feel like it.

DOLLY: All right, if you don't feel like it, you can help me clean this place up. Looks like a flamin' rubbish tip.

[*She hands the broom to* MEENA.]

MEENA: Aw Mum, I'm goin' out.

DOLLY: What, with them Yorlah girls again?

MEENA: No I'm not, as a matter of fact, I'm not.

DOLLY: I saw the youngest one down the car park and she was drunk, drunk as a monkey.

MEENA: Well, that's her, not me.

DOLLY: I dunno why you can't get some decent friends instead of those barefooted blackfellas you muck around with all the time.

MEENA: I don't muck around with them all the time. I said I wasn't going out with them, didn't I?

DOLLY: Who are you going out with, then?

MEENA: Ross.

DOLLY: Ross, Ross Mumblin?

MEENA: Yeah.

DOLLY: Where are you goin'?

MEENA: To the drive-in.

DOLLY: What are you goin' to see?

MEENA: [*shrugging her shoulders*] I dunno.

DOLLY: Why don't you get yourself a decent boyfriend like Robert?

MEENA: Aw Mum, he's my cousin.

DOLLY: I know that, but somebody like him. He's gotta good job, nice car.

MEENA: What's wrong with Ross's car? He's got a V8 panel van and he's done it up real nice, got an airconditioner, stereo, bed and . . . and . . .

DOLLY: Yeah, I bet he has. You make sure you're home by ten o'clock.

MEENA: Ma-am, the pictures don't finish till after eleven.

DOLLY: You be home by 11.30.

MEENA: Oh gawd, I don't know what you got against Ross, Mum. He doesn't even drink.

DOLLY: It's not the drink I'm worried about. Look, I seen girls, young girls, younger than you walkin' around with babies on their hips and I don't want that happening to you, my girl.

MEENA: Aw Mum, what do you think I am, a slow learner or something?

DOLLY: I don't, but you've had a pretty fair crack of the whip and it's time I started puttin' my foot down.

MEENA: Uh-ah!

DOLLY: You been comin' home late at nights far too often the last couple of months.

MEENA: I haven't done anything wrong.

DOLLY: I didn't say you had, but I notice you're always too bloody tired for school next day.

MEENA: Aw Mum, why can't I leave school, anyway?

DOLLY: What do you want to leave school for? So you can lay around doin' nothing? You're goin' to school for another two years, you can get that into your head.

MEENA: I'm not gonna lay about. I'm gonna get a job, Mum.

DOLLY: What sort of a job are you going to get? In the supermarket, in a factory? Look, you've got enough brains to get a good job, you're smart in school, you get good marks, good reports. You could stay on at school and get an Aboriginal study grant and really make something of yourself.

MEENA: Like what?

DOLLY: Get a decent office job, or become a nurse.

[WORRU *appears in the doorway, jacket off, coughing painfully, a pitiful sight in his grubby singlet, baggy trousers and bare feet.*]

Hullo, Uncle, how are you?

[*He sways precariously. She jumps up and runs to his aid.*]

Oh gawd, Meena, help him.

[*They gently shepherd him across the room and into a chair.*]

MEENA: Come on, Pop, steady.

WORRU: [*to* DOLLY] No good, *warrah, nitjal koong minditj.*

DOLLY: How long has he been like this?

MEENA: Oh he's been OK. He just seems to get sick night time.

DOLLY: Go and get a blanket for him. You feel cold, Uncle?

[*No reply.*]

Noonuk gnitiung?

WORRU: Ugh . . . yeah.

[MEENA *returns with the blanket and carefully drapes it over his shoulders. She walks over and collects her jeans from in front of the radiator and moves the radiator closer to* WORRU.]

MEENA: I'm gettin' ready.

[*She exits to her room.*]

DOLLY: Like an orange, Uncle? All the way from Sawyers Valley, lovely and sweet.

[*He feebly puts out his hand, she gives him an orange. He sits there holding it.*]

I seen old Harold up in Northam.

WORRU: *Winjar?*

DOLLY: In Northam, poor old Harold, [*holding her palm at the level of her stomach*] he got a *gnarnuk* down here.

WORRU: Ah, he's only young fella.

[*He laughs and coughs.*]

I kick his arse when he was a little fella.

[*They both laugh, his laugh becomes a nasty cough. She puts a handkerchief to his mouth, then takes the orange from him firmly.*]

DOLLY: Gimme that, Unc. I cut it up for you, it'll stop you from coughing. Hey Unc, you get your pension next week and I'm gonna buy you some singlets, new ones to keep you warm. You want white ones or black ones?

WORRU: Black ones, like me.

DOLLY: And we'll get you some new hankies.

WORRU: *Kia*, white ones.

[DOLLY *laughs.*]

Next week I go to Pinjarra.

DOLLY: What for?

WORRU: See *Nyoongah* doctor.

DOLLY: Yeah, good idea, I'll get Robert to drive us down there.

[WORRU *eats a piece of orange.* DOLLY *unsuccessfully searches for food.* MEENA *appears dressed to go out.*]

MEENA: Mum, you got any money, couple of dollars?

[DOLLY *searches in her purse and hands* MEENA *one dollar.*]

DOLLY: I'll give you a dollar, it's all I got to spare. Gotta buy tucker, can't depend on your father to bring anything home.

MEENA: Bye Pop, bye Mum.

DOLLY: Midnight, remember.

MEENA: OK.

[MEENA *leaves, walks across the stage and exits.* WORRU *attempts another piece of orange but gives up. It falls into his lap.*]

DOLLY: Ay Uncle, you feel all right?

WORRU: Yeah, I'm all right, I go *gnoorndiny*.

DOLLY: [*lifting him*] Yeah, come on Uncle, you go and lay down.

[*She guides him to his room.*]

I'm going down the shop to get some *merrany* and *dytje*. You have a sleep, I'll bring your supper in later.

[*She puts him to bed, covers him up and returns to the kitchen. She turns off the radiator, collects her handbag and leaves. As she walks across the stage counting her money,* WORRU *begins mumbling to himself, gradually building to a disturbed cry.*]

WORRU: Milbart, *Winjar Noonuk*? Make a *kaal*. *Gnuny gnitiung. Witjar gnank weerdiny*, Milbart. *Gnuny* wanta *kaal koong dookan gnoordiny*. Milbart *yuarl nyinaliny gnoor-*

diny. Milbart *yuarl nyinaliny gnullarah.* Milbart *kaal wah.*
(Milbart, where are you? Make a fire. I'm cold and the
sun is going down. I want to lie with my side to the
fire. Milbart, are you coming to lie down with me?
Milbart, come here to me. Milbart, make a fire.')
> [*Didjeridoo crashes in, the lights change. The* DANCER
> *appears at front of stage and in stylised rhythmic steps
> searches for stone flints, finds them, builds and ignites a
> fire. Carefully he lifts the fire in cupped hands and carries
> it to the escarpment where he blows it gently, igniting a
> careful fire, and sits warming himself against a dark night
> sky as the music climaxes and cuts.*]

SCENE TWO

A short while later WORRU *is home alone, sleeping in his room.
Offstage in the distance* ELI *can be heard singing 'Onward
Christian Soldiers'.*

*He appears, sways drunkenly across the stage, stops and
attempts to count his money. Notes and coins extracted from
various pockets fall on the floor. He nearly topples over as he
picks them up.*

ELI: Ten dollars and eighty one cents! Not bad, old
Hawkeye, not bad at all.
> [*He pulls his eye patch down and addresses an imaginery
> passer-by.*]
Got bad eyes, boss, this one got catarac', this one goin'
fast. Can you spare forty cents, boss? God bless you,
sir, God bless you, missus. [*Gesturing skywards*] Hey!
Big boss! You up there! You listenin'? Hope you been
givin' out some of them blessin's I been promisin' them
wetjalas.
> [*He removes the eyepatch, puts it in his pocket and heads
> for the house singing 'Onward Christian Soldiers'. He
> enters the house and looks about.*]

Hey! Anybody 'ome? Anybody 'ome? I bet them blokes slipped me up on purpose.

[*He drops into a chair and tears the wrapping from a flagon of VO invalid port and downs a drink.*]

Well, they don't know I got this. [*Singing*] Onward Christian Soldiers, marching on —

[*He stops abruptly.*]

Ay? 'ow can you be a soldier an' a Christian? Lot a rot; soldiers used to chuck Christians to the lions. I'm a Christian, Freo Prison Christian. Ain't nobody gonna chuck me to the lions. The *Wetjala's* a lion, he eats. Aw, he eats, he eats everything: land, trees, rivers, forests, even people, 'specially people. I 'member old grandfather Kooroop used to say: 'Don't trust the *Wetjala*, he's a real *widartji*. He'll kill you for sport and eat your brains and kidney fat.' Poor old grandfather.

[ROY *enters and walks across the stage carrying a flagon.* ELI *pours another mug of port and begins singing 'Yes, Jesus loves me'.* ROY *enters,* ELI *attempts to hide his flagon under the table.*]

ROY: Nobody lubs you. Anyway, what did you leave me for?

[ROY *pours himself a drink.*]

ELI: I never left you, you left me. [*Holding out his mug*] Pour me a drink.

ROY: Why?

ELI: 'Cause I want a drink.

ROY: What's that under the table?

ELI: That's a flagon of VO. I'm savin' that for us later.

ROY: Ah, this is good ol' Valencia.

[ROY *pushes the flagon across to* ELI *and takes out a packet of tailor-made cigarettes and fumbles about unsuccessfully for matches.*]

Give us the matches.

ELI: Ain't got any.

[ROY *stumbles across to the sink, looks for matches, and spots* DOLLY's *suitcase.*]

ROY: Jesus!

ELI: What?

    [ROY *gestures at the suitcase.*]

  Oh, Lawd.

ROY: She musta went down the street.

ELI: [*staring at his watch*] Northam bus only just gettin' in.

ROY: She musta gotta lift.

ELI: Who with?

ROY: Musta been one of Elaine's boys.

ELI: Not that smart arse, Robert?

    [WORRU *wakes, sits up suddenly and cries out.*]

WORRU: Ay! Ay! Milbart! *Winjar noonuk!*

ROY: Go and see what he wants.

ELI: He's got a good nose, that old fella, he smelt this.

    [ELI *goes to* WORRU's *room.* WORRU *drops on to his bed and mumbles to himself.*]

WORRU: Milbart, *yuarl nyinaliny gnullarah.*

ELI: Ay old fella, you all right.

    [WORRU *grunts and coughs.*]

  Ay, Unc, you want a *kaep?*

WORRU: No, *yuart.*

ELI: What, you *minditj*, Uncle?

WORRU: Yeah, no good, no good, I go Pinjarra tomorrow, me and Dolly.

ELI: Yeah, what you goin' there for, Uncle, gunna see some of your old girlfriends?

WORRU: [*dropping off to sleep*] Go Pinjarra, see *Nyoongah* doctor.

ELI: Sure, Uncle, you have a *gnoorndiny* now, Aunty Dolly be 'ome drecktly.

    [*He returns to the kitchen.*]

  'E's still talkin' about the *Nyoongah* doctor, lotta bullshit.

ROY: I dunno, might do him some good.

ELI: Balls.

ROY: Don't worry about that, I seen some good things done by some of them fellas.

ELI: Yeah, what?

ROY: Once them *nyoongahs* was fightin' on the six acre reserve at the Williams' and old Morden got his 'ead split open with a *doak* an' Yinell, he was *boolya* man, he got some of that green slimy stuff from the river and packed it all around 'is 'ead and he was good as ever. [*Laughing, miming a boxer*] He come back lookin' for more of this.

[DOLLY *enters and walks across the stage carrying a small bag of groceries.* ELI *fills the mugs.*]

ELI: I still reckon it's a lotta bullshit.

ROY: *Nyoongahs* never went to *Wetjala* doctors in them days. They was frightened of 'em.

ELI: Yeah, that's why so many of 'em fuckin' died.

[DOLLY *enters, stops in the doorway and surveys the scene.* ROY *does his best to appear sober.*]

ROY: Aw, 'ullo love, 'ow you goin'? Didn't know you was' 'ome.

ELI: Yeah, spotted your bag.

ROY: [*to* ELI] Shut up! [*to* DOLLY] 'E's drunk.

DOLLY: [*putting the groceries away*] Same old homecomin'.

ROY: 'Ow d'ya get 'ere, on the bus?

DOLLY: No, Robert brought me 'ome.

ELI: I thought so.

ROY: Has 'e gone back?

DOLLY: No.

ELI: [*under his breath*] Worse luck.

DOLLY He took Shane to footy practice.

[DOLLY *goes through her suitcase.*]

ROY: 'Ow's Peter?

DOLLY: Aw, 'es all right, he's puttin' on weight. 'Ere, he sent this for you.

[*She presents him with a fancy leather stubby holder.*]

Made it himself, it's a stubby holder.

ELI: Shoulda been a flagon 'older.

ROY: Well, 'e'd 'ave to make you one too.

ELI: Gawd I'm hungry. What's for supper, Auntie?

DOLLY: You're gettin' polony sandwiches.

[DOLLY *strides across to* ROY, *puts her hand out and flips her fingers.*]

Come on, come on, you know what: *boondah*.

[ELI *laughs,* DOLLY *turns on him.*]

You too, Eli. [*To* ROY] Come on, come on, stand up.
[ROY *stands. She goes through his pockets.*]

ELI: You got more pockets than a pool table.
[DOLLY *counts the money.*]

DOLLY: You shut up, Eli, your turn next. Ah, sixty bucks, wonders will never cease.

ROY: [*laughing*] Ha, ha, you missed one, you missed one.

DOLLY: Come on, come on, how much you got in it, come on, how much?
[ROY *produces a dollar.*]
You can keep that.
[*She turns on* ELI *and puts out her hand.*]

ELI: You won't have to search me, Auntie, I'm as honest as the day is long.

DOLLY: Come on, Eli, forty, come on.
[*She dips her hand into his pocket.*]

ELI: Ay, Auntie, no, *choo*, this one's Patchy, this one SS pocket.
[*A car is heard pulling up, doors shut.* ROBERT *and* SHANE *enter and walk across the stage.* SHANE *has a football and* ROBERT *a carton of beer.*]

DOLLY: I don't care which pockets you get it out of as long as I get it.
[ELI *reluctantly produces a handful of notes which he drops.* DOLLY *scoops them up quickly.*]
Ah, that's rent and tucker for the next coupla weeks, anyway.
[DOLLY *stuffs the money down her bra.* ROBERT *and* SHANE *enter the house.*]

ROY: Ay, 'ow you goin' neph'?

ROBERT: Good, Unc, how are you?

ROY: I'm OK.

SHANE: What's for supper?

DOLLY: I'm makin' sandwiches drecktly. Gawd, look at you. You better go and have a shower, you're filthy.

ROBERT: [*to* ELI] How are you, Eli?

ELI: Aw, not bad.

SHANE: Aw Mum, I couldn't do a thing right at practice, I got dumped every time.

ROBERT: Don't worry, mate, I told you everybody has their off days.

ELI: Ah, you should 'ave me for a coach.

[ROBERT *and* SHANE *are playing handball.*]

ROY: [*pensively*] Dinkum?

ELI: Look, I tell you, I played full forward for Federals in Wagin. One match I kicked ten goals, right through the big sticks.

[*He demonstrates.*]

ROY: Full forward. [*Laughing*] Full and forward, belly up to the bar and then you got kicked right outa the pub.

ELI: OK. Give us it here, I'll show you how to handle a football. Come on, come on, punch it 'ere, come on, punch it 'ere.

SHANE: Right. Lead, cousin Eli, lead!

[SHANE *punches the ball to him hard. It hits him in the stomach, he falls awkwardly, winded. Everyone laughs.*]

ELI: [*puffing*] Ay, ay, fair go. I wasn't ready, come on, come on.

[*He sets it up to punch it back but* ROBERT *flicks it out of his hand.* ELI *raises his hand to strike him.*]

DOLLY: All right, come on you boys, steady down.

SHANE: Give us the ball.

DOLLY: I'll have the ball before youse break something.

[ROBERT *passes the ball to* DOLLY.]

SHANE: Put it under my bed, Mum, I'm gonna have a shower.

[*He exits.*]

ROBERT: [*to* ELI] You couldn't get a kick in a stampede.

ELI: Yeah? I was the only one what gave the scoreboard fellas cramp.

ROBERT: Must have been from laughing at not changing the scores.

[WORRU *suddenly lets out a mournful wail.*]

WORRU: Ay, Dulong, Benyi, Winarn, coooo — ooh!

DOLLY: Oh Lawd.

[*They all stand transfixed looking towards his room.*]

ROBERT: I'll have a look, Auntie.

[ROBERT *runs into* WORRU's *room.* DOLLY *follows.* WORRU
appears to be asleep.]

You OK, Uncle?

DOLLY: Uncle Worru, you all right?

ROBERT: He's asleep.

[DOLLY *puts a blanket over him, they return.*]

ROY: What's up with him?

DOLLY: I dunno, must 'ave been talkin' in his sleep.

ROBERT: He's OK.

DOLLY: He reckons he wants to go to Pinjarra next week.

ROBERT: What for?

DOLLY: He wants to see the *boolya* man.

ROBERT: Don't worry Auntie, I'll drive you down there.

ELI: Waste of fuckin' petrol money, if you ask me.

ROBERT: I'll be paying for the petrol, not you.

ELI: Why don't you take him up here where you been
takin' him for the last four or five years?

DOLLY: They'll only keep him there. You know how he
hates hospitals.

ELI: I still reckon he's better off in hospital than someone
mumblin' a lot of blackfella bullshit over him.

ROBERT: Can't you see the old bloke believes in it? It's
not going to do him any harm. It's faith healing, purely
a case of mind over matter, auto-suggestion. Call it
what you like.

ELI: You call it what you like, I call it bullshit.

DOLLY: [*to* ELI] Pipe down, you.

ROY: [*laughing*] Let 'em go, let 'em go.

ROBERT: Now you take the Bible, the story of Noah's Ark.
It would have been physically impossible for Noah to
transport every species of animal on earth for forty
days and forty nights.

ROY: Oh, that's my nephew. You're solid, neph'. Keep
goin', keep goin'.

ROBERT: [*pointing at* ELI] And to prove it even more —

ELI: [*knocking his hand*] Don't you fuckin' point at me.

[*He twists* ROBERT'*s finger.*]

ROBERT: [*stepping back*] To prove it even more, Noah would have had to have a staff of thousands to feed all those animals and look after them.

ELI: Yeah, well you listen, you think you know everything. What about them big boats come into Fremantle? They take thousands of sheeps and take 'em to other countries. If those fellas can do it, Noah coulda done it.

ROBERT: The point is because thousands of people for thousands of years have believed in the story of Noah's Ark, they believe through faith. You see what I mean, Auntie?

DOLLY: [*uncertainly*] Yeah.

ROY: Well, I don't.

ELI: He's talkin' out of his *kwon*. If it's in the Bible it's bloody true.

ROBERT: Listen coz, belief in the Bible is based on faith, not fact.

[*He points,* ELI *grabs his finger and twists it hard.*]
Hey! Cut it out.

ELI: I told you not to point, didn't I? [*Twisting it viciously*] Didn't I?

ROY: Come on, cut it out, cut it out.

DOLLY: That'll do! That'll do! Stop it, you two.

[WORRU *sits up and lets out another harrowing wail.*]

WORRU: Milbart, coooo—oooh!

[ELI *lets go of* ROBERT'*s finger.*]

ROY: Lawd, not again.

[DOLLY *runs to his room.*]

WORRU: Benyi, plenty *yongarah* there, Milbart? Fresh water? [*Laughing heartily*] *Woolah!* I come *boordah-woon, kia, kia.*

DOLLY: Ay, Uncle?

WORRU: What?

DOLLY: You all right?

WORRU: Yeah, I'm good.

DOLLY: You lay down, cover yourself up.

WORRU: Nah, I'm goin' drecktly.

DOLLY: Where you goin'?

WORRU: That-a-awy, *bo-oh-oh*.

ROBERT: Is he OK?

DOLLY: Yeah, he reckons he's takin' off drecktly.

ROY: You wanta watch him, love, he might do that.

DOLLY: Nah, he'll go back to sleep now.

ELI: Tie him up, Auntie, one leg to the bed.

ROBERT: That's the sort of thing you would say.

ELI: I'm only jokin'. You wanta stop gettin' heavy, mate.

  [ROBERT *replies with the 'up yours' gesture.*]

ROY: He'd get loose, he's a cruel strong old man.

DOLLY: Old Uncle Harold was tellin' me a story about
  oldy, when he was a young bloke workin' on Minilya.
  The overseer and the boss tied him up and they belted
  him and belted him with a bleedin' stock whip and
  they left him there tied up in the sun. Anyway he got
  loose and night time they was *tjurip* sleepin', he snuck
  up on 'em and he belted them two *Wetjalas* somethin'
  cruel.

ROBERT: What happened, did they catch up with him?

DOLLY: No way. Old Harold reckon he done that.

  [DOLLY *gives the* Nyoongah *gesture for running off.*
  SHANE *appears from the shower with a towel over his
  shoulders. He makes for the radiator.*]

  You go and get a shirt on.

SHANE: I'm OK.

DOLLY: Go on, you gotta cold already.

SHANE: If I can find a clean one.

WORRU: [*calling*] Hey, hey! Shane? Shane boy, come 'ere.

DOLLY: [*to* SHANE] Go and see what he wants. [*To* WORRU]
  He's comin', Uncle.

  [ELI *produces a pack of cards.* SHANE *goes to* WORRU's
  room.]

ELI: Who wants a game?

ROY: OK. How much a hand?

SHANE: What did you want, Popeye?

ELI: [*to* ROBERT] I don't suppose you play cards?

WORRU: Where you been?

ROBERT: I can reef your money off you any day, mate.
[DOLLY *throws a blanket over the table. They sit down and commence the game.*]

SHANE: I just had a shower.

ROY: Right, twenty cents jackpot.

SHANE: Eh, Popeye, you look funny sittin' there. Here, I'll comb your hair.

WORRU: You wanna watch out, don't go thatta way.

SHANE: [*laughing*] Yeah, why?

WORRU You go thissa way, I seen them featherfoot tracks there. Aha, they think they clever fellas, not as clever as me.

SHANE: Yeah, that's right, Popeye, that's right. You lay down.

WORRU: You watch out now.
[SHANE *returns.*]

SHANE: Aw Mum, he's talkin' about feather foots.

DOLLY: Aw, he's been dreamin'.

WORRU: Ay! Ay! Shane, Shane! Come 'ere, come 'ere. Where you is?

SHANE: [*exhaustedly*] Oh no, not again.

DOLLY: Go on, talk to him, I'll bring both youse supper in as soon as I've reefed a dollar off your father.
[*She laughs.*]

SHANE: All right, I'm comin', Popeye.
[SHANE *walks in and sits down beside the old man.*]

DOLLY: And Patchy's money off cousin Eli.
[*The card game continues in earnest.* WORRU *claps his hands.*]

WORRU: *Gnuny* gonna sing 'bout them *tjenna guppi.*

SHANE: Yeah, Popeye.

[*As he sings, clapsticks followed by didjeridoo take up the rhythm. The light fades on the kitchen, then on* WORRU's *room.*]

WORRU:

Allewah! Tjenna guppi nyinanliny,
A nyinanliny, a nyinanliny, nyinanliny,
Mundika Nyinanliny,
Mundika nyinaliny,
Ngunyinniny kaka woorniny,
A kaka woorniny,
Tjenna guppi nyinanliny,
Tjenna guppi,
Tjenna guppi,
Tjenna guppi,
Woolah!

['Watch out, featherfoot there
There, there, there
There in the bushes
There in the bushes
I'm laughing
Laughing
Featherfoot there
Featherfoot
Featherfoot
Featherfoot
Hooray!']

[*Shafts of cold light fade in revealing* THE DANCER *as featherfoot at the front of stage. He is heavily decorated with leaves and carries two short sticks. He dances slowly across the stage and up on to the escarpment and off as the music and lights fade.*]

SCENE THREE

A few hours later SHANE *is asleep on the foot of* WORRU's *bed. The card game continues, empty cans litter the table.*

ELI: I'll bet a dollar.

ROBERT: OK. I'm looking.

DOLLY: I'll have a look.

ROY: [*throwing in his cards*] That's busted me. I'm gonna settle down to some steady drinkin'.
    [*He picks up a flagon and sways across to the couch.* ELI *triumphantly shows his cards.*]

ELI: Three fives!

DOLLY: That beats me.
    [ELI *reaches for the money,* ROBERT *grabs him firmly by the hand.*]

ROBERT: Hold it, hold it coz, three sixes!

DOLLY: Gee, that was a good pot.

ELI: Bastard! Give us the cards.

ROY: Started on Patchy's pocket yet nephew?
    [ELI *shuffles the pack.*]

ELI: Bloody cards, oughta be chucked in the bloody fire.

ROBERT: You can please yourself, they're your cards. Anyway I'm thirty dollars in front.

ELI: Bully for you. Anyway, it's early yet.

ROBERT: Right, your deal.
    [ELI *shuffles furiously and drops several cards. As he picks them up he slips a few cards, unseen, under his leg.*]

DOLLY: Come on, you two. Stop snapping at each other. You're like two cats.

ROY: More like two *dwerts*. Eli's a kangaroo dog and Robert's a greyhound.

ELI: Right, who's got openers?

ROBERT: Not me.

DOLLY: No, not me.

ELI: Right, I'll open it for two dollars.

DOLLY: I'm out.

ROBERT: [*to* ELI] You got a pat hand?

ELI: I'm not gonna tell you.

ROBERT: You have to.

ELI: I don't.

ROBERT: He has too, doesn't he, Uncle Roy?

ROY: Don't put me into it, I'm not playing.

ROBERT: That's the rules.

ELI: Look, we're playin' jackpot *Nyoongah* way, not *Wetjala* way.

ROBERT: All right, give me four cards.

ELI: Sure, my little greyhound of a cousin.

ROBERT: All right, all right, what do you bet?

ELI: You want to bet, eh? All right, five dollars!
   [*They each throw in five dollars.* ELI *goes to put his cards down.*]

ROBERT: Wait a bit, wait a bit. Back another five dollars.

ELI: Aha, cheeky bugger, eh? Your five.
   [ELI *stands up and goes through his pockets.*]

DOLLY: Eh, you boys are getting a bit heavy.

ROY: Eh Mum, don't forget to take the light money out of this pot.
   [ELI *throws a handful of notes and coins into the pot.*]

ELI: And back seven forty! And you can't kick it again 'cause that's all I bloody well got. Aha, beat that, three tens and a pair of nines.
   [ELI *throws his cards down triumphanty.* ROBERT *stands and shows his cards one after another.*]

ROBERT: One, two, three, four sevens. I don't care whether you're playing *Nyoongah* way or *Wetjala* way, four cards beats a full hand anytime.

ELI: Fuck the cards, lend me five bucks.

ROBERT: What for?

ELI: Lend me five bucks.

ROBERT: Here you are. I don't mind collecting it out of your next SS.

ELI: Right, come on, come on!
   [ROBERT *deals.*]

DOLLY: Well leave me out, I never lost anything. I finished up square.

ROY: I only lost a dollar.

DOLLY: Yeah, and what I gave ya, don't forget that.

[*While* ROBERT *is dealing* ELI *drops his cards and as he picks them up attempts to substitute some for the ones he is sitting on.* ROBERT *sees him. He stands up and reaches across the table grabbing* ELI *by the shirt.*]

ROBERT: Eli, you fucking, cheating, black bastard.

DOLLY: Oh, Eli.

ELI: What's bugging you?

[ELI *grabs for the pot but* ROBERT *beats him to it.* ELI *grabs* ROBERT *by the wrist and jerks him violently over the table. Chairs, cards and beer cans go flying.* ROBERT *grabs* ELI *by the hair,* ELI *tries to kick him.*]

You got my money there; come on hand it over.

[DOLLY *tries to break up the fight,* ROY *tries to rescue the booze and during the chaos* WORRU *falls off his bed.*]

SHANE: Mum, Mum!

ROBERT: I haven't, you stupid idiot.

DOLLY: Stop it, stop it you two!

SHANE: [*entering in a panic*] Mum, Dad!

ROBERT: You fucking cheat.

DOLLY: Will you stop it?

SHANE: Popeye's sick!

ROBERT: I lent you five dollars, you ungrateful bastard.

SHANE: Help Mum, Popeye's sick!

[DOLLY *runs into* WORRU's *room. The fight continues.*]

ELI: Let go of my hair. Fight like a man, not a bloody woman.

ROBERT: You fight like a bloody horse.

[ELI *manages to kick* ROBERT *hard in the leg.* ROBERT *pulls away,* SHANE *runs between them crying hysterically.*]

SHANE: Stop fightin'! Popeye's fallen off the bed.

[*The scene freezes.*

The light changes, didgeridoo crashes in a wild threatening drone: The DANCER, *again as featherfoot, appears and moves slowly across in front of them removing the decorating leaves and leaving them strewn on the front of the stage. As he exits, the sound and light fades.*]

SCENE FOUR

A distant ambulance siren, the hollow footsteps and clatter of a hospital corridor. A pool of light reveals WORRU, *wrapped in a blanket, sitting in a wheelchair.* DOLLY *stands beside him.* WORRU *looks about vaguely.*

WORRU: Where's everybody?

DOLLY: They're all home, Uncle.

WORRU: *Yuart*, somebody was 'ere.

DOLLY: That was Robert, Uncle.

WORRU: Where's he gone?

DOLLY: He's talking to Sister, filling in some forms for you.

WORRU: [*trying to get up*] I'm not staying here!

DOLLY: [*restraining him gently*] You just stay here for a little while. Next week I take you to Pinjarra.

WORRU: No, I'm goin' that way.

DOLLY: You'll be all right Uncle. Doctor's coming to see you drecktly.

WORRU: Hm! Who's that fella?

DOLLY: What fella, Uncle?

WORRU: [*impatiently*] That *Nyoongah* fella! Bring us here.

DOLLY: Oh Uncle, that's Robert, he's one a' your grannies. He's one of Elaine's boys. They used to stay with us at Grass Valley. You 'member?

WORRU: I know, I know, Grass Valley, all got sent Mogumber.

DOLLY: No, that was before, Uncle, that was *koora*.

WORRU: Yeah, big mob, all go to Mogumber, big mob, 'ad to walk. Toodjay, Yarawindi, New Norcia. Summertime too. Can't go back to Northam, no *Nyoongahs*. *Kia*. I runned away with Melba. [*Laughing*] Jumped the train at Gillingarra. Went back to Northam, [*miming handcuffs*] *manadtj* got me at the Northam Show. Put me in gaol, Fremantle, for long time. When I went back to settlement Roy was born, [*gesturing*] this big, *kia*, [*laughing*] little fella.

[*He laughs and begins to cough painfully.* DOLLY *comforts him.*]

DOLLY: You talkin' too much, Uncle, you sit quiet now.
[*He holds* DOLLY *tight by the arm.*]
You sit quiet now Uncle, I'm stayin' right here.
[*A nurse enters, looks at* DOLLY *and slowly wheels* WORRU *off.* DOLLY *follows.* WORRU *mumbles to himself as the lights fade.*]

WORRU: Milbart, Dulung, Benyi, Winarn, Milbart, Milbart.

SCENE FIVE

A few hours later SHANE *is asleep on the couch.* ROY *is sitting staring blankly into space.* ELI *is on his hands and knees clearing up.*

ELI: What a bloody mess.

ROY: You made it, man, you made it.

ELI: I didn't do it all on me bloody own.
[SHANE *stirs and turns over on the couch. A car is heard pulling up outside. One door slams.* SHANE *jumps up half asleep and runs across to the sink and peers out.*]
That must be them.

SHANE: No it isn't.

ROY: Who is it?

SHANE: Oh, its only Meena.
[MEENA *walks across the front of the stage. Her hair and clothes are dishevelled. She puts her shoes on and attempts to tidy herself up.*]
She'll cop it when Mum gets home.

ROY: She deserves all she bloody well gets.
[MEENA *creeps silently into the house and stops bewildered.*]

MEENA: Where's Mum?

ROY: Where have you been?

MEENA: Is she in bed?

SHANE: No.

ROY: Do you know what time it is?

MEENA: [*ignoring him*] Where is she, then?

SHANE: Her and Robert took Popeye to the hospital.

MEENA: What for?

ELI: Aw, he got crook.

MEENA: Is he all right?

SHANE: Popeye got a fright and fell out of bed.

ROY: Anyway, where have you been? It must be two o'clock in the bloody morning.

MEENA: To the drive-in.

ROY: Till this hour of the morning?

MEENA: We run out of petrol.

ROY: How did you get home, then?

MEENA: Ross's car.

ROY: Thought you said you run out of petrol.

MEENA: We did, but we got some off Jimmy Yoolah.

ROY: You'll need a better excuse than that when your Mother gets home. Have you got enough energy to make me a cup of tea?

MEENA: Aw Pop, I'm tired. I gotta get up and go to school in the morning.

ELI: [*getting up and putting the pot on*] Useless, bloody useless.

ROY: A good clip in the ears would do you the world of good, young lady.

MEENA: You know what's wrong with you, Pop, you got a hang-over.

[*She nestles on to the couch next to* SHANE.]

SHANE: Don't take all the blankets.

MEENA: Gimme some.

SHANE: Aargh, keep the stinkin' blanket.

[*He grabs the cushions, makes a bed on the floor and goes to get a blanket from* WORRU'S *bed.*]

ROY: Why don't you go and get in your own bed?

MEENA: I'm sittin' up till Mum and Popeye get home.

[SHANE *runs from* WORRU'S *room dragging the blanket behind him. He stops, alarmed, and looks behind. They all look at him in silence.*]

ELI: What's wrong?

SHANE: Ooh!

[SHANE *stands there and looks at them.*]

MEENA: What's up?

SHANE: Something in there.

MEENA: Where?

SHANE: In Popeye's room.

ELI: Ah, you seein' things.

[SHANE *wraps himself in the blanket and curls up on his makeshift bed.*]

ROY: Shane, why don't you go to bed?

SHANE: I'm not goin' till I find out how Popeye is.

[ROY *walks slowly out to* WORRU'S *room.*]

ELI: Aw, stop worryin', boy, you couldn't kill that old fella with the back of a sleeper axe.

[ROY *stands still in* WORRU'S *room, then walks back with slow measured steps, all eyes are on him.*]

What's the matter?

[ROY *looks at him, doesn't reply but sits and stares blankly ahead.*]

MEENA: What time is it?

ELI: About half past two. You want a cuppa tea?

MEENA: No, I wanta sleep. Wake me up when they get home.

[ELI *makes a cup of tea.* SHANE *covers his head with the blanket, the lights fade slowly.*

A narrow shaft of light reveals the DANCER *sitting cross-legged on the escarpment against a night sky. He sings sorrowfully.*]

> *Nitja Wetjala, warrah, warrah!*
> *Gnullarah dumbart noychwa.*
> *Noychwa, noychwa, noychwa.*
> *Wetjala kie-e-ny gnullarah dumbart.*
> *Kie-e-ny, kie-e-ny, kie-e-ny,*
> *Kie-e-ny.*

> ['The White man is evil, evil!
> My people are dead.
> Dead, dead, dead.
> The white man kill my people.
> Kill, kill, kill,
> Kill.']

SCENE SIX

A few hours later the first light of dawn silhouettes the house. SHANE *and* MEENA *are asleep.* ROY *is dozing in a chair and* ELI *stares blankly out the window.*

Eventually a car is heard pulling up outside. Two doors close. ROY *wakes. A distant didjeridoo drone begins as* DOLLY, *followed by* ROBERT, *walks slowly across the stage.* DOLLY *is carrying* WORRU'S *clothes. The didjeridoo builds as they enter the house. They stand in silence.* ROY *and* ELI *stare at* DOLLY *hopelessly.* DOLLY *puts the clothes on the table, walks across to the couch and wakes* MEENA. ROY *goes to* MEENA. SHANE *stirs, wakes and looks about.*

SHANE: Where's Popeye?
    [DOLLY *kneels beside him, whispers in his ear and holds him in her arms. He cries out, the didjeridoo builds to a climax and cuts. Blackout.*]

SCENE SEVEN

A single shaft of light reveals DOLLY *alone centre stage. She speaks slowly with restrained emotion.*

DOLLY:

        Stark and white the hospital ward
        In the morning sunlight gleaming,
        But you are back in the *moodgah* now
        Back on the path of your Dreaming.

        I looked at him, then back through the
           years,
        Then knew what I had to remember:
        A young man, straight as wattle spears
        And a kangaroo hunt in September.

We caught the scent of the 'roos on the
    rise
Where the gums grew on the Moore.
They leapt away in loud surprise
But Worru was fast and as sure.

He threw me the fire-stick, oh what a
    thrill!
With a leap he sprang to a run.
He met the doe on the top of the hill
And he looked like a king in the sun.

The wattle spear flashed in the evening
    light,
The kangaroo fell at his feet.
How I danced and I yelled with all my might
As I thought of the warm red meat.

We camped that night on a bed of reeds
With a million stars a-gleaming.
He told me the tales of *Nyoongah* deeds
When the world first woke from
    dreaming.

He sang me a song, I clapped my hands,
He fashioned a needle of bone.
He drew designs in the river sands,
He sharpened his spear on a stone.

I will let you dream—dream on old friend
Of a child and a man in September,
Of hills and stars and the river's bend;
Alas, that is all to remember.

[*Blackout.*]

THE END

NOTES AND GLOSSARY OF ABORIGINAL TERMS

The Aboriginal language used in these plays is usually called *Nyoongah* but occasionally referred to as *Bibbulumun*. *Nyoongah* literally means 'man', but has become a general term denoting Aboriginality in the South-West of Western Australia. *Bibbulmun* is one of the fourteen South-West languages that have combined over the last 152 years to create the modern *Nyoongah* spoken in the play.

ALLEWAH, watch out!
BAAL, them
BAHKININY, bite
BANTJI, banksia
BARMINY, strike
BEEYOL, river
BITJARRA, sleep
BOH-OH, a long way
BOK, skin cape, also clothes
BOOLYA, magic
BOOLYADUK, one skilled in magic
BOONDAH, money; literally, stone
BOONDAH WAH, do you have money?
BOORDAH WOON, soon, directly
BOORL, BOORL, rifle or musket, derived from the sound of shots
BOOTJARI, pregnant
BRIDAIRA, boss, master
BUKILY, hit
BUNJIN, play around (with women)
CHOO, shame
CHOO KIENYA, real shame
DALYANINY, run away
DOAK, throwing stick
DOMJUM, Aboriginal man described in the Perth *Gazette* as Yagan's brother
DOOGEEARKINY, flee
DOOKAN, lying on one's side
DOUBLEGEE, a clover burr prevalent in Western Australia
DUBBAKINY, slowly
DUMBART, people of the same tribe
DWERT, dingo, dog

DYTJE, meat

GIDTJI WAH, do you have a spear?

GILGY, known as yabbies in the Eastern states; a small, fresh-water crustacean. A corruption of *'tjilki'*

GITJUL, spear

GNANK, sun

GNARNUK, beard

GNITIUNG, old term for a white man, lit. cold

GNOOP, blood, also wine

GNOORNDINY, sleep

GNOWANGERUP, a South-West country town

GNULLARAH, ours

GNUMMARI, a mild, narcotic root; tobacco

GNUNY, me, I

GOONAMIA, toilet; literally excrement shelter

GUPPI, feathers

JAM, tree of W.A., *acacia acuminata*

JINNA, feet

JUNGARA, returned dead. The Tjuart believed that when they died their *kanya* (freshly departed soul) rested in the *moord-gah* tree (*nuylsia floribunda* or Christmas tree) until it departed for *Watjerup* (Rottnest Island) when the tree's vivid orange blossoms die. There it shed its dark skin and appeared white. When Captain Stirling and his party landed, the Aborigines assumed them to be the *jungara* ('the returned'). They assumed the visit of the *jungara* was temporary; some even recognised departed relatives. They were surprised, however, that the visitors had forgotten their names, their language and their law.

KAAL, fire

KAAL WAH, do you have fire?

KAEP, water

KAEP WAH, do you have water, liquor?

KARBUL, fish

KARDA, racehorse goanna

KARGATTUP, the area surrounding *Karta Koomba*

KARLAWOORLINY, hot

KARTA KOOMBA, Mount Eliza, literally 'head that is huge'. As the highest point in an area surrounded by marshes, plains and the Swan River, with a running freshwater spring at its foot, *Karta Koomba* was probably an important site to the Tjuart clan that occupied the region. Recent excavations have revealed middens several metres below the surface.

KARTWARRAH, mad, bad in the head
KEERT KOOLINY, going quickly
KIA KIA, yes yes
KIENY, ill
KOBBLE, stomach
KOBBLE WEERT, hungry
KOHN, wild potato
KOOLBAHRDI, magpie
KOOLINY, go
KOOLONG, KOOLONGARAH, child, children
KOOLYAMUT, lie
KOOLYUWAH, one who tells lies
KOOMBAHINY, huge
KOOMP, urine
KOONG, side, rib cage
KOORAM, long time, before
KOORAWOORLINY, an expression of disbelief
KOORI, term denoting Aboriginality in N.S.W. and Victoria
KUDDEN, red gum tree
KULKANA, mullet
KULLARK, home
KULUMAN, *(coolamon)*, basin-shaped wooden dish
KUNARN, the truth
KUNYA, a freshly departed spirit
KWIPPINY, stealing
KWOBINYARN, excellent
KWON, arse
KWOTJUT, in the past
KWOTJUT NOYCH, dead a long time
KYLIE, boomerang
KYNYA, shame
LAKE GEORGE HILLS site of a massacre near Canberra
MAHMBOYET, mouth of a river
MAHNGK, leaves, vegetation, tea
MAHRI, clouds
MANATJ, police, literally 'black cockatoo'. The dark peak-cap
    uniforms of the early police caused them to be compared
    to this bird.
MARTA, legs
MCLARTY'S RUN, the McLartys were a substantial land-owning
    family in the Pinjarra region
MEOWL, eye
MEOWL BIRT, blind person

MERRANY, damper, flour, bread

MIDDAR, traditional dance

MINDITJ, sick

MIRROLGAH, balance, the act of throwing a spear

MITJITJIROO, (d. 1833), possibly a tribal father of Yagàn

MOBYRNE, magic

MOODGAH, *nuystia floribunda*, West Australian Christmas tree

MOORDITJ, good

MOORE RIVER, the Mogumber Native Settlement, a State Government Reserve established in 1918 and closed in 1951.

MOORLIE, unkind spirit

MOORLIN, back

MOORLY, nose

MOORNAWOOLING, black

MOYARAHN, term denoting status roughly equivalent to that of a grandmother

MURRAY TRIBE, a reference to the Battle of Pinjarra on the Murray River

MUTTLEGAHRUK, sand plain tree

NIETJUK, who

NITJAL, here

NOONINY, NOONUK, you

NOP, boy

NOYCH, NOYCHWA, dead

NUMBER NINES (coll.), big feet, police

NUNBULY BUKULY, round and round, continually hitting

NYINALINY, there

NYINNING, here

NYNGARN, echidna

NYOONDIAK, brains

NYOONGAH, Aboriginal, literally 'man' in the languages of the South West. Some time after 1829 it entered common usage as a term denoting Aboriginality, similar to *Wongai* in the eastern goldfields, *Yamatji* in the Murchison and *Koori* and *Murri* in the eastern states.

NYOORNDITJ, a pitiful person

NYORN, pity

OORAWOORLING, destitute, having nothing

NYUMBY, traditional dance

TJARRALY, jarrah

TJEN KOOLINY, walk

TJENNA, feet

TJENNA GUPPI, featherfoot, executioner

TJENNUK, unkind spirit

TJINAHNGINY, look

TJINAHNG, see

TJOPPUL, plop

TJUELARA, skinny

TJURIP, pleased

UNNA, isn't it?

WAHNGING, talk

WAHRABBINY, rolling

WAHRDUNG and KOOLBAHRDI, one of the few surviving legends of the South West, literally 'The Crow and the Magpie'. This version was passed on to the author by his stepfather, Bert (Kurrahtj) Bennel, in the early 1930s.

WAHNA, woman's digging stick

WARRGUL, the rainbow serpent, creative spirit of the Swan River, *Warrgul* moved over the land, creating the Darling Ranges and the Swan Valley before resting at *Kargallup* (corrupted to *Karrakatta*, now Perth)

WARRAH, bad

WARRAMUT, bad

WARRAH WANGEING, bad mouthing

WART ARNY YIT, move along

WATJERUP, Rottnest Island

WAYARNING, frightened

WEERDINY, downwards

WETJALA, white person, a corruption of the English 'white fellow'

WIDARTJI, an evil spirit

WINJAR, WINJAR KOORL, which way, which way are we going?

WINJAR NOONUK, where are you?

WINYARN, weak-willed person

WIRILO, curlow, derived from that bird's haunting nocturnal cry; used also as an expression of grief

WOOLAH, a shout of praise

WONGAI term denoting Aboriginality in the Eastern goldfields

WOONANA, behind bars

WOORT BEERNY, to strangle

WORRARRA, a tribe massacred in the Kimberleys as retribution for the murder of two white men while laying the overland telephone line

WUH WUH, greetings

YAGAN, (d. 1833) a totemic name meaning 'freshwater turtle'.
Yagan was assumed by Captain Stirling to be a tribal leader.
He learned English rapidly and, showing a flair for diplomacy, he negotiated with Stirling. When agreements were
broken he led a guerilla-style campaign of resistance and
retribution until his death. Now he is an important symbolic
figure for the *Nyoongah*

YAHLLARAH, a traditional dance

YAMATJI, term denoting Aboriginality in Murchison and Gascoyne regions; lit. friend

YIMMUNG, forehead

YIRRKALA, the Aboriginal tribe that lodged the first land claim
in the white man's court. The tribe took the Comalco Company to court contesting the Commonwealth Government's
action which allowed Comalco to mine Aboriginal land.
The Yirrkala lost the case.

YOK, woman

YONGA, YONGARAH, kangaroo

YORGA, woman

YORLAH, the Yorlahs are a fictional family, however the experiences of Thomas are based on those of a number of
Aboriginal people involved in the 1933 northern transfer

YUARL, you

YUART, no

YURON, bobtail goanna

MURRAS

Margaret Hayes as Ruby, David Page as Wilba, Adelaide Fringe
Festival production. Photo: Di Barrett.

Above: Jillian Karpany as Jayda, Muriel Van Der Byl as Granny. Below: Steven Page as the Mimi and Muriel Van Der Byl. Adelaide production. Photos: Di Barrett.

Steven Page as the Mimi. Adelaide Fringe Festival production.
Photo: Di Barrett.

Murras opened at the Fringe Festival Centre during the Adelaide Festival in March 1988, with the following cast:

RUBY	Margaret Hayes
GRANNY	Muriel Van Der Byl
WILBA	David Page
JAYDA	Jillian Karpany
RUSSEL MITCHELL	Michael Fuller
THE DANCER/	
THE MIMI	Steven Page

Directed by Eva Johnson
Designed by Cath Cantlon
Lighting and set design by Sue Grey Gardner

CHARACTERS

MIMI SPIRIT, a dancer
GRANNY, an elderly woman
RUBY, the mother, in her twenties
WILBA, her thirteen-year-old son
JAYDA, her sixteen-year-old daughter
MR RUSSEL, Department of Aboriginal Affairs worker, in his late twenties

SETTING

This play focuses on one family and their struggle to come to grips with white Australia as they move from fringe dwelling to life in the city. The action takes place between the late sixties and mid-seventies, a time which saw the beginning of changes to laws relating to Aborigines, including the abolition of the Aborigines Protection Board.

NOTE

Mimi is a mythical being that inhabits certain parts of the country. It can be the spirit of a dead ancestor, sometimes friendly, sometimes hostile, and the Mimi dance is very much a part of the traditional dances performed today. Mimi is a very powerful spirit who can generate magic to bring about sickness and death. It is the caretaker of the dead spirit.

ACT ONE

SCENE ONE

The MIMI SPIRIT *sits in a coiled position before the Great Rainbow Serpent motif. The didjeridu begins to play and the* MIMI SPIRIT *wakes and slides across the stage, awakening the earth spirits. This is the birth dance of the Aboriginal Dreaming. The dance ends in darkness. Blackout while props are brought on: a door, a window, an old car seat. A transistor on the window sill plays the song 'I Don't Want to Play House.' Fade up. Enter* RUBY, *carrying a bath tub. She places it on top of a kero tin and begins to wash clothes. When the song ends the ABC News is introduced.*

ANNOUNCER: [*voice over*] This is the ABC News read by Charles Drury. There has been evidence in recent years of increasing consciousness of the rights of the Aboriginal Australian. Commonwealth and state ministers stated that: 'The policy of assimilation seeks that persons of Aboriginal descent will choose to attain a similar manner and standard of living to that of other Australians and live as members of a single Australian community, and we believe that if Aboriginal Australians can be helped and encouraged to help themselves, then they will be readily attracted to and welcomed to the assimilation we aim for. Therefore, new housing will be allocated for them in different towns and cities. The Minister further commented that the move to the cities will —
　　[RUBY *angrily switches the transistor off.*]
RUBY: [*to the radio*] Don't talk like that. We don't wanna go, what for? No good, I tell you.
　　[*She returns to her washing.*]
Better live here outside. We got no doors to lock out family. Look, look my *murras*.
　　[*She raises her hands out of the water.*]
All time work hard, dig for yams, make fire, make basket, dilly bag, pandana mat . . . and carving.

[*She looks at Charlie's totem, centrestage.*]

Charlie, you were the best carver. Your *murras* were strong, you was the best. What I'm gonna do, Charlie? I can't leave my country. What I'm gonna do . . . ?

[*She is interrupted by her son,* WILBA, *who enters and goes to the door, carrying a pile of wood and a bucket of water.*]

WILBA: Mum, Mum, open the door; this bucket real heavy. Got some more wood, too, and good feed of yabbies.

RUBY: [*letting him in*] Well, put that bucket down there, but get them yabbies out; we gotta drink that water. Anyway, what you doin' home from school? You gotta go to that school, Wilba, else them Government fellas come check up on us.

WILBA: I hate that school, Mum, true as God. I hate that school. Always gettin' into trouble for nothing. *wudjellas* make me real mad: I all time flog them. Call me 'Abo', 'boong', 'nigger', and all time dirty names. I'm not goin' back, Mum, true as God, I hate that school.

RUBY: Well, it probably don't matter now: we leavin' this place, anyway.

WILBA: What you saying? Mum, where? What place? Who told you?

RUBY: I heard, just now. On the wireless. Government fullas talking about new houses for Aborigines in the city.

WILBA: No way, not me. I'm not going nowhere, I ain't; just stay here and be good stockman like my father and do carving and go hunting with Jumbo.

RUBY: We gotta do what they tell us, you know that. Jumbo was good friend of your father, Wilba.

WILBA: [*looking at the sculpture*] Yeah, he use to watch my father carve; he showed Jumbo how to ride, track, hunt and dance . . . What he have to die for, Mum? What did my father have to die, what he drink that *wudjellas* drink for, make him sick, make him die?

RUBY: Your father died because he lost his land, everything. But he never forgot how to carve, hunt and dance. But plenty more dyin', Wilba, plenty more. Dyin' here inside, for their land. When you got nothing, all you want to do is die.

WILBA: [*sadly, picking up the totem*] He taught me to dance the moon dance. Taught me to carve emu eggs. Mum, he was too good to die, he didn't hurt no one.

RUBY: You keep his dance, his spirit, Wilba. You are the shadow of your father. He always say you be like him. Oh, my God, I almost forget: Sister coming today. She probably want check you over too. Come on now, take this — water still hot. Go give yourself good clean up.

WILBA: What Sister want to check me for? She think I got germs, all time put that purple paint on me. I got no ringworm, *doolum*. No nothing.

[RUBY *hands* WILBA *the tub and pushes him out the door. He sticks his head in the window and yells out.*]

Mum, look here: Granny and Jayda coming.

[*He exits.* GRANNY *and* JAYDA *enter.* GRANNY *has a walking stick.*]

RUBY: Where you two been? Sister coming, gotta clean up. Here, Jayda, hang these clothes up.

[GRANNY *sits on the car seat.* RUBY *sits by the fire to make her a cup of tea in the billy.* JAYDA *starts hanging out the clothes on a piece of string tied from the door to the window.*]

JAYDA: Mum, I thought I saw Wilba with bath tub. Don't tell me he's gonna clean up. Probably tip that water out, just wet his hair, put powder on him, just gammon have wash, aye?

RUBY: Jayda, you gotta clean up too. Sister always see you. Granny, you real quiet. You alright?

GRANNY: No, I'm not alright. Everybody leavin' this place. Jessie, Tom, they gone now, gone to city. Left yesterday. That fulla from Government reckons we all be leaving, but they just wanna try move me, I'll —

RUBY: [*interrupting*] You mean that Mr Morton from Welfare? Granny, he right, you know. I heard them on the wireless talkin', just *wudjellas* telling us what's good for us.

GRANNY: He was tellin' all of them mob at the Kimberly reserve. Jumbo took me up to see Jessie, dropped us off just now. But he gone further up; he not goin' city, me neither. I

born here, I die here, this my born place. They don't wanna
try move me, I'll give it to 'em, true as God.

RUBY: Granny, we all stay together. We take care of you. Anyway, you not gonna die, you tough like old buffalo.

JAYDA: Here, Granny, have cuppa tea.

[*She sits by* GRANNY's *feet.*]

You want your pipe? Give me your string bag, I'll fix it.
Granny, you gotta teach me more dance; anyway, you been
here the longest, they can't move you. You belong this
country.

GRANNY: I seen too many things changing. Too many people
dyin' from wrong ways. Moving about too much, disturbin'
the land. My Charlie, they move him from his land, to
station, to creek bed. He finish there, in creek bed. No
good, I tell you. No, something happening our people.
Soon we all gone. Something happening, I tell you, no
good.

RUBY: Nothing gonna happen; they know what's good for us.
You'll be alright, Granny, as long as we take plendy
pandana, talc stone and emu eggs. And you can still teach
Jayda to dance.

JAYDA: It's gonna be different, Mum, I know. I work for that
wudjella woman in town and I know. Sometimes she follows
me around while I clean up. And she just sit and stares at
me, make me eat my lunch outside. She belts her children
if they talk to me. I'm not gonna work for no *wudjellas* in
city, that's for sure.

GRANNY: *Wudjella* woman got different way to *gadjeri* woman.
They don't have woman's dreaming, special dance, *Inma*.
Jayda, you not forget your stories now. You keep them
sacred, for your children, not *wudjellas*.

JAYDA: Mum, what was that fulla sayin' on the wireless?

RUBY: Well, that fulla reading the news just said something
about Aborigines being Australians. Minister from
Government saying that we should all move to the city so
we can be same as white fullas. And I remember that Mr
Morton calling us 'fringe dwellers' or something. People
who live between the city and their own land, I think. Our

land been taken over by that cattle station, so they have to
find houses for us. I don't want to go, but too many dying.
Maybe it's better for us.

GRANNY: You can't leave Charlie. You know that, Ruby.

[GRANNY *stands and moves forward.*]

[*Softly*]

You know who we are;
Yeah, you, Ruby, you are dugong,
Charlie, he moon,
Wilba, he parrotfish,
Jayda, she seagrass,
Me, I'm from water.

Dreaming say, dugong was bitten by leech.
Moon watch her.
Dugong leave her land and go into sea.
Moon follow, but he can't get wet,
So he call parrotfish, make him son.
Parrotfish look after dugong.
Both live from seagrass from bottom of the sea.
Moon always there, watch all time.
And he here, still he look for you, dugong.
Water, dugong, parrotfish, seagrass,
All same spirit, so we gotta stay together, right
here.

RUBY: Charlie gone back to his Dreaming. He alright.

JAYDA: That our Dreaming. We will all return to the sea,
except my father, he is moon. I'll see if I can see the moon,
sometimes I talk to . . .

RUBY: Sit down! Sit down, Jayda. I know it's not the same
now, everything is changing. All different. But we will
come back here one day, just like Charlie. We will come
back in our one time. Back to our Dreaming.

GRANNY: Ruby, Jayda learn a new dance; you want to see her?
Come on, Jayda, do little dance for your mother.

JAYDA: You want me to, Mum?

RUBY: Yes, my baby, do a little dance for me.

[JAYDA *dances for a short while.* WILBA *peeps through the window and watches. There is a knock.* JAYDA *stops dancing and sits by* GRANNY. *Enter* WILBA.]

WILBA: Mum, someone here to see us.

RUBY: Well, let him in.

[*Enter* RUSSEL MITCHELL, *an Aboriginal liaison officer.*]

RUSSEL: Hello, my name is Russel Mitchell, and you must be Mrs Francis.

RUBY: Yes, and this is my mother Elsie, my son Wilba and my daughter Jayda.

WILBA: You hear about Mum's new house? We heard about it, everybody movin' to the city.

RUSSEL: Yes. My God, look at this place. I mean, how long have you been living like this? I mean here?

RUBY: We've been here a few years now. We lived on a station till Charlie lost his job. Then Mr Morton got us this place after Charlie died.

RUSSEL: Charlie. That's your husband?

RUBY: Yes, he died from too much —

WILBA: [*interrupting*] Mum! You don't have to tell him all that.

RUSSEL: Oh, it's alright, I understand. We are all the same.

JAYDA: Mum, you don't really have to, you know. Charlie's gone now. You don't have to talk about him.

RUBY: He died from too much grog. Well, that's what they said. They used to come in cars and sell it to us, flagons of grog. They made lot of money, too. That wasn't what really killed him.

GRANNY: He was the best carver: look there. He never forgot who he was; not my Charlie. He was hungry for the land. They stole it from him. He was best carver, only wanted to live blackfella way.

WILBA: He carved totem poles, for ceremony, tall ones, and strong. His *murras* were strong, had to be to carve totems.

GRANNY: No, we not the same. You ever lived in the creek bed, Mr Russ? You sleep in sand with the sky for your blanket. Hear what the wind say to you in your sleep and what the birds' call mean at night?

RUSSEL: No, well I don't really know. But I'm sorry for your husband, Mrs Francis. I'm sorry, it's not my business.

RUBY: Where you come from, Mr Russel? You look like you . . .

RUSSEL: [*interrupting*] What I'd like to talk to you about is your new home. It's very modern, you'll notice the difference. It has electricity. Yes, you can't see it, but it's there. It's like magic; it provides power for lights, heaters, washing machines, refrigerators, almost anything. You won't hardly have to use your hands.

WILBA: '*Murras*'.

RUBY: We call them '*murras*'.

RUSSEL: What? Electricity?

JAYDA: No, these hands, our '*murras*'.

RUSSEL: '*Murras*'. Yes, well as I was saying, everything will be at your fingertips.

WILBA: As long as I can still go hunting, paint and make spears.

JAYDA: And weave baskets and mats and —

RUSSEL: [*interrupting*] You can join classes, yes, there are classes for everything these days. Look, I did: now I do my own banking, book-keeping and I can chair meetings and run seminars.

RUBY: Why does the Government want to give us a house in city?

RUSSEL: To improve your housing conditions. To enable you to live a normal life. To better yourselves.

GRANNY: But we like it just the way it is out here, how it always is.

RUSSEL: There are lots of Aborigines moving to the cities.

RUBY: Where did you say your country was?

RUSSEL: Wilba, can I see some of your carvings, please?

[WILBA *takes an emu egg to* RUSSEL.]

WILBA: This an emu egg. See, the trees, the kangaroo. Still got a lot to do yet.

RUBY: [*to* RUSSEL] Who your mother? Who your father? Where did you say you from?

RUSSEL: [*examining the egg*] There's been a lot of work put into this. The design is so intricate. You are very clever, Wilba. I could never do anything like this.

WILBA: You could if we teach you, aye, Mum?

RUSSEL: No, this is something you grow up with. It's been passed down from generation to generation. I should be able to but . . . Mrs Francis, you keep asking me where my country is. I don't know. I had an Aboriginal mother, but I was taken away. I was adopted to a white family when I was two.

RUBY: I could see you was a little *nungar*.

RUSSEL: There was that policy that took all half-caste children from their tribal mothers. I was on a mission, but I don't remember, I was too young.

GRANNY: They still doin' that now, mothers hidin' their babies. Covering them up with ash to make them look full-blood.

RUSSEL: They are kind to me — my adopted parents, they give me almost everything I want. I've had a good Christian education, a good home and a job. I haven't really missed out on much in life.

RUBY: But you are nothing if you don't know where you come from.

RUSSEL: I wanted to find out once, but now I'm married and have a family of my own. I'm happy with my life, and this job enables me to help other Aborigines that haven't had what I have.

GRANNY: That's why you got this job? You never know, you might be our relation, aye?

RUSSEL: Yes. Well you see, the Department thought that it would be easier for you people to talk to an Aborigine rather than a European. They call it self-determination. We are helping our own people, and seen as positive role models for you.

JAYDA: Will the Department give me a job?

RUSSEL: Maybe, in a hospital or working for a family.

JAYDA: See, I told you mum, working for *wudjellas* again.

WILBA: You ever been hunting? Come on then, take off them clothes and put real proper clothes on and I'll take you out now to find emu eggs, what you reckon?

RUSSEL: I really haven't got time now, as I have other calls to make.

RUBY: What's gonna happen to this land? It still belongs to our people?

RUSSEL: No, there's to be a new highway put in here and a swimming pool close by for the townspeople.

GRANNY: They just move us around like cattle. Why don't you tell them we want stay here, we not . . .

RUSSEL: I have to make my report and I'll tell them for you, but I'm sure that when you see your new home you will probably change your mind.

RUBY: We don't understand about this report business, but we do what they tell us. You want cuppa tea, Mr Rus?

RUSSEL: Russel, just Russel. Yes, please.

[JAYDA *pours tea for all.*]

Jesus, just look at this place. How can you live here? No running water, ceiling must leak in the wet, and probably bloody cold in winter. Just look at this dirt floor, it's a breeding ground for rats and diseases; a real health hazard.

WILBA: We get water in bucket from pipeline half mile down the track, that's if they don't turn it off first. But when we have good rain, plenty water in creek, and yabbies too, aye.

GRANNY: Long time, before pipeline, river all time had water. Then cattle come, big dam come, dry 'em up all creek, water hole. Mess 'em up country real proper way.

JAYDA: [*to* RUSSEL] Your cup of tea, Mum likes it real strong; add some powdered milk if you want.

RUSSEL: Thank you. Well, I hope the referendum improves things for you. Just think, it's nineteen sixty-seven now, and in twenty years' time these places will no longer exist. They will have been abolished and we can look back on this very day. That's what the referendum means: self-determination for Aboriginal people, and a better way of life.

RUBY: Russel, you gotta find your people, you know that? They probably look for you all this time.

RUSSEL: [*standing*] Yes, well, that's something I have to think

about. I'm glad to have met you, Mrs Francis, and I will do
my best to make your transition to the city easy for you. I
really must go now, other calls to make. Goodbye, everyone. And thank you for the cup of tea.

[*He exits.* GRANNY *angrily hits her stick on the ground.*]

GRANNY: I'm not leavin, I tell you. I born here, I die here. No
one gonna move me from this place, true as God, no one.

WILBA: I'm stayin' with you, Granny.

RUBY: It'll be different, we'll be real flash, aye?

WILBA: Mum, that fella, Russel, he reckon he got everything,
aye, but I feel sorry for that fella. He never been in the
bush. Funny for a *nungar* to get scared of the bush, aye?

RUBY: He find his mother, one day, he know he gotta. Plenty
get taken from their people, but find them later on. Well, I
better get ready for Sister now. Come on, help tidy up. I'll
go wash up.

[RUBY *moves to the door.*]

GRANNY: Hang on, Ruby. I better come too.

RUBY: No, Granny; Sister don't want to see you.

GRANNY: I don't wanna see Sister, I wanna go Goonawalli.
Else I'm in biggest trouble.

[GRANNY *and* RUBY *exit.*]

WILBA: [*sitting by fire carving*] Hey Jayda, what was that dance
you was doin' when I come in?

JAYDA: Wilba, you not allowed to look at that dance, you
cheeky, lookin' at me. Mum flog you if she finds out.

WILBA: No, she won't. I can dance too, you know.

JAYDA: Come on, show me then. You can't dance, aye?

[WILBA *gets up.*]

WILBA: This dance my father taught me. There he is: moon
man, standing by sea looking for dugong. See her and he
do this dance for her.

[WILBA *dances for two or three minutes, circling* JAYDA. *She rises
slowly and joins in until the two are dancing. They dance towards
the totem where the dance ends with a blackout.*]

END OF ACT ONE

ACT TWO

SCENE ONE

RUBY *packs clothes, plates, incidentals into an old tea-chest.* GRANNY *smokes her pipe while weaving a mat.*

RUBY: Where that Wilba? I don't like him going out with them mustering mob. Them fullas no good, all time hungry for woman. Fill 'em up with grog. Mr Morton told them to stay away from this place.

GRANNY: School no good for Wilba. He better stockman, bushman. He gone looking for ride, to help out.

RUBY: What you gonna take to city, Mum? You want me to pack for you?

GRANNY: Never mine me Ruby, I be alright. Ain't got much, anyway. Dillybag, pipe, tobacco. What that Sister say to you yesterday, Ruby?

RUBY: Nothing, she say I'm alright. Just gave me a bit of sugar, tea and more kero. Couldn't find that Wilba. He took off from her. She went and seen Jayda at that *wudjella's* place.

GRANNY: I don't blame him. Wilba — takin' off from her. He hates that paint, reckon he can't get it off for days. Make him look like blue-tongue lizard. Poor fulla.

RUBY: Sister don't say much anyway, just write in her book all the time. She sticky beak, ask questions about Jayda. Don't tell her nothing, but.

GRANNY: Well when you go to city, you still have welfare come check up on you, you know. No good, I tell you.

[*As* RUBY *talks, the sound of horses galloping can be heard, first faintly, gradually becoming louder.*]

RUBY: Charlie went to the city once, I remember . . . what's that? Some important fulla got one of his totems for . . . what's that, horses? . . . for museum . . . horses and screaming. Watch out, that might be Jayda.

[RUBY *runs to the door, opens it, and* JAYDA *falls into her arms. She is shaken, hysterical, trying to talk and panting.*]

RUBY: Jayda, what happened? Who, what they done . . .

[JAYDA *collapses into* GRANNY's *lap.*]

JAYDA: Mum, it's alright. They didn't catch us.

[RUBY *runs from door to window, looks out and shouts.*]

RUBY: You bastards, you keep away from here you filthy hungry dogs. You hear, you *wudjella* bastards? I'll get you for this.

JAYDA: They chased Jessie and me. We was walking home from doing ironing. They was coming from the hotel way. We heard them whistle and we took off.

RUBY: What about Jessie? She alright?

JAYDA: I don't know, she went one way, I took off this way. They caught up with us, on their horses. I got a stone and hit one bloke in the eye. He got real mad and ripped my dress. Said he was gonna . . .

GRANNY: Shhh! Don't you talk too much my baby. You alright, just lie down and forget about it.

RUBY: [*picking up a stick and walking towards the door*] I'm gonna go find those dogs, I'll flog them, no one gonna touch my children. I better find Wilba too.

GRANNY: No, Ruby, here you stay with Jayda, I'll find Wilba and Jessie. And those fullas don't want to muck around with me they'll be sorry, true as God, plenty sorry. I'll give it to 'em.

[GRANNY *exits.* RUBY *comforts* JAYDA. *She wipes* JAYDA's *face with a damp rag.*]

JAYDA: Mum, I'm sorry.

RUBY: Not your fault! Now you listen Jayda, this is not your fault. Don't you take shame for those filthy *wudjellas*. Everything alright, you rest, my baby.

[RUBY *moves away from* JAYDA, *crouches by the fire and looks at the totem as if talking to Charlie once again.*]

Charlie, they mess'n' up our country, puttin' shame on our children. They got no law, no shame. They no good. I'm goin', I'm goin', take Jayda away from here. They killin' our dreaming places, no good . . .

[WILBA *enters, followed by* GRANNY.]

WILBA: Mum, I heard screaming, and horses galloping. I was with Jumbo down by the creek, when Jessie come up running, crying, screaming. Jumbo took off after them fullas, he got them mum, gave them biggest floggin! He gone now, taking Jessie back home. What about Jayda? She alright? Jayda?

RUBY: She alright. Granny you stay here with her. I'll go find Mr Morton, he can take us to police station. Wilba, you come with me.

WILBA: Don't go police, mum. They won't do anything, just throw Jumbo in jail, that's all.

RUBY: We be back soon Granny.

[RUBY *and* WILBA *exit.*]

GRANNY: [*softly*] Jayda, your mother, she wild like wounded buffalo, but she fix up everything. *Wudjella* don't know our lore, they got no spirit. They don't have one time, like us, don't have dreaming. They nothing people, Jayda, nothing people. Jayda, listen now, I teach you one more time. Soon my time coming.

JAYDA: Granny, don't say that.

GRANNY: Shhh! Soon my time coming; no more for me to do. I seen lot a things happening, some good, but mostly bad. You know they tried to take Charlie away from me. One *wudjella* man wanted me, for himself. I told him I gave him away to 'nother woman. But I hid him, hid him in my sugar bag. I was nearly sittin' on top of him while I was lyin' to that *wudjella*. He was a good boy, kept real quiet. I kept hidin' him, until he met your mother. Hm, well, soon I'll find his spirit again. And Jayda . . . Jayda . . . you sleep? My little sea-grass, my little sea-grass. You listen for me, I sing to you, you listen now . . .

[*The lights fade softly to black.* GRANNY *hums to* JAYDA.]

SCENE TWO

GRANNY's *dying scene. This scene symbolises her return to the earth and the traditional preparation of her body to return to the spiritual world of her dreaming, returning to her ancestors. The mimi spirit is there to return her safely by dancing around her, calling her back into her world, her time.* GRANNY *sits in the centre of the motif, swaying, rocking to and fro, wailing as she gathers handfuls of sand and gently pours them over herself. After the dance of the spirit is completed, he encapsulates her by stretching over her, engulfing her. This is done to the music of the didjeridu and clapping sticks. At the end of the dance, the lights slowly fade until the stage is totally black.*

SCENE THREE

Slow fade up. The sounds of the bush can be heard. RUBY, WILBA *and* JAYDA *enter and slowly gather all their belongings. Then they hear a bulldozer, off. The family exits.* JAYDA *runs back on.*

JAYDA: [*calling*] Granny! Granny!
　　　[*She realises that* GRANNY *has gone. Blackout.*]

END OF ACT TWO

ACT THREE

SCENE ONE

The year is 1970. The family have moved to the city. JAYDA *is a domestic in a hospital and* WILBA *is finishing school.* JAYDA *vacuums the living room floor.* WILBA *enters with a Coke in his hand and a schoolbag. He flings the bag across the floor in anger, then sits on the sofa with his head down.*

JAYDA: [*switching off Hoover*] What's up?

WILBA: Nothing, I'm alright.

JAYDA: No you not, come on, Wilba. You look real mad. Look at you. Alright, if you won't tell me.
    [*She switches the Hoover on.*]

WILBA: Alright, alright, I'll tell you.
    [JAYDA *switches the Hoover off again.*]

JAYDA: I know something's up.

WILBA: I got into trouble with headmaster. Got the cane.

JAYDA: What for this time. Fightin' again?

WILBA: I don't care, next time I'll flatten him real proper way. This fulla called me a filthy nigger, abo bastard. Aldo told him to shut up, but he got his face punched in.

JAYDA: Aldo always stick up for you.

WILBA: Yeah, that's why I joined in. I wasn't gonna let him get into trouble over me, so I dropped that fulla.

JAYDA: What did you do to him?

WILBA: Only gave him a black eye, blood nose. Should have laid him out, true as God, should have.

JAYDA: Well the three of you deserve that cane, fighting like that.
    [JAYDA *unplugs the Hoover and rolls the cord up.*]

WILBA: What you talking about, Jayda? I was the only one got the cane. That *wudjella* headmaster make me real mad. He goes . . . 'You have to learn to behave. We can't have you acting like a nomad down here.'

JAYDA: Now listen Wilba, it's not that different for me, either.
I work in the kitchen with Russians, Italians, Greeks, you
name it, but I'm the only Aboriginal, and boy do I get it.
All the dirty jobs, bossed around, and I got to stop myself
from getting mad. I don't want to lose my job so I just walk
away.

WILBA: Not me, I'm gonna fight.

JAYDA: It's because we different, they don't understand us.
They never seen blackfullas before, probably scared of us.
They'd die if they had to live in the bush like us. Come on
Wilba, don't let them kill us.

WILBA: I'm not going tomorrow, I'll make out I'm sick or
something.

JAYDA: Don't do that, that won't help. You just gotta be best at
the things you can do. You the best runner, footballer,
drawer, aren't you? Well just . . . shhh! That must be
Mum.

[RUBY *enters carrying a bag of clothes. She flops onto the sofa.*]

RUBY: Hullo, I'm buggered, phew. These *boogadies* hurt my
feet.

JAYDA: Mum, you been spendin' up real good, looks like.

RUBY: Just been to the mission. Jessie and me been driving
around dropping off clothes to other *nungar* families. Got
few for you two. Look in there now.

[WILBA *opens the bag and spreads the clothes out on the floor.*]

WILBA: Wow, look here, jumper, jeans, socks, and look here,
gundies, real neat, aye?

JAYDA: That jumper looks good on you, Wilba, and look here,
this dress real pretty, but too small for you, aye Mum?

RUBY: [*standing and picking up the dress*] No Jayda, this dress I
got specially for you, to wear to Jessie and Tom's tomorrow
when —

JAYDA: [*angry and loud*] Mum, I told you before. I'm working
now and I can buy my own clothes. I can't wear anything
like this. Shame job.

RUBY: What, you too good now? I always got clothes from
there before. You didn't say anything then.

JAYDA: It's not that. I have to dress the same as . . .

WILBA: Mum, I think I'll go watch TV at Aldo's. See youse later.

[*Exit* WILBA.]

JAYDA: It's not that, Mum. I have to dress the same as my friends. I've got to be the same, Mum, or they'll laugh at me.

RUBY: Laugh, aye? You should be the one laughing, Jayda. You listen here, I'm not too shame. Let them think we different. I'll take them for everything they gotta offer. Jayda, it's *them* they *want* to treat us like this. I'll take them for every hand-out, ration, free pass, for every penny. As long as they *don't* think we like them, we sittin' pretty.

JAYDA: But you deserve brand-new clothes, not hand-me-downs. You will always be nobody if you let them treat you like that. Don't you see, Mum?

RUBY: When you got no money for brand-new clothes, you have to feel proud in any clothes. I'm not too shame, Jessie not too shame, I know lot of *nungars* not too shame.

JAYDA: They don't like it if you act like blackfulla, either. Sometimes I gotta be better, dress better, everything better than them. I can't be different, Mum.

RUBY: I'm same person in old dress like I am in brand-new dress. I don't change. But you, Jayda, you changin', gettin' new ways. You didn't want to come city, remember? You want to go back now, Jayda? They all gone, Jayda, our people all gone.

JAYDA: I have changed, Mum, I'm older, I'm different now.

RUBY: You don't make baskets no more.

JAYDA: [*grabbing the basket hanging on the wall*] There's no place for baskets here. It doesn't mean anything to them . . .

RUBY: It doesn't have to! [*She grabs the basket from* JAYDA.] This belongs to you! *This* you gotta teach your children one day.

RUBY: When you get married you will, and that's whe —

JAYDA: I can't have children, Mum.

RUBY: What? What you saying, Jayda? Who told you that?

JAYDA: Doctor at the hospital, I had a medical, a test, he told me.

RUBY: Medical? Test? What for?

JAYDA: It was a routine check-up. The doctor called me in one day. He had some special papers there, he said they were from the government, said that I was part of a programme or something, long time ago. Had to do with those injections that Sister use to give me and Jessie.

RUBY: Injections? You didn't tell me about any injections.

JAYDA: Mum, she said it was alright. I thought you knew, she said she explained it to you. She told me it was to stop diseases.

RUBY: She lied. Injections to stop disease, injections to stop babies. They lied to us, who they think they are? Boss over you, boss over me — your mother?

JAYDA: Mum, it was an experiment. We can't do anything about it now. Mum, I'm alright, it's alright.

RUBY: No, it's not alright! Jayda, you was only fourteen years old, still my baby. What kind of law they got? They mess around with our women's business, they bring death to our land, shame to our children . . .

JAYDA: I saw a woman from Welfare, she said there's nothing I can do. But I thought of being a nurse, Mum, and going back to make sure they still not doing this.

RUBY: Those filthy *wudjella* dogs, they knew who had those injections. That's why they chased you and Jessie.

JAYDA: How would they know, Mum? We never spoke to them.

RUBY: I remember, I remember that Sister coming around mustering time. She use to drink with them in the pub, that's how they knew.

JAYDA: Mum, come here. Remember when Granny said *wudjella* woman got different way to *gadjeri* woman? They don't have woman's dreaming, special dance, *Inma*. Then she said, 'Jayda, you not forget your stories now, you keep them sacred for your children, not *wudjella*.' Granny call them nothing people, got no spirit.

RUBY: They all nothing people. Granny and I teach you your own women's business. And that Sister, she take everything away from us.

JAYDA: No, Mum, no one take you from me, or Granny.

Mum, sit down, I get you a cup of tea. Mum, I'll be a good
nurse, you wait and see. You be real proud of me. I gotta go
back to work. You be alright?

[*She gathers her bag for work and sits beside her mother.*]
Don't worry about me . . . I'll be alright. I love you, Mum,
I love you.

END OF ACT THREE

ACT FOUR

It is some years later. WILBA *is now a black activist for the Aboriginal land rights struggle which has swept the nation. There have been marches in all capital cities, and a rally which resulted in the Aboriginal Tent Embassy being set up on the lawns of Parliament House in Canberra.* WILBA *is often arrested in these protests.*

RUBY *sits on the sofa watching T.V.* WILBA *enters, and quietly sneaks up behind his mother, startling her.*

RUBY: Wilba, Wilba, what you doing home? I've been watching you on T.V. You alright? Want something to eat?

WILBA: Thank you, Mum, but I'm not staying. Just getting few clothes, blankets, on my way through.

RUBY: Through to where? Where you going?

WILBA: Mum, car outside, I'm in a hurry.

RUBY: I haven't seen you for a long time. Stay and have talk, come on, Wilba.

WILBA: Mum, I don't have time, I tell you, gotta go.
[WILBA *fills clothes into a land rights bag as he talks to his mother.*]

RUBY: Wilba, you alright? Something wrong?

WILBA: I've had a gutful of this place. They got bulldozers going up, bloody bulldozers, Mum, on our land. No way no fuckin' mining company's gonna dig up my father's bones, our burial grounds.

RUBY: They can't do that, that's sacred place. They can't do that. Charlie, and Granny they . . .

WILBA: You better believe it, they are.

RUBY: What you gonna do? What can you do, Wilba? Don't go gettin' yourself into trouble, now.

WILBA: We gonna march, Mum. Hundreds of us, not just me. We all going up there to sit on that land when the trucks and bulldozers come in. Those politicians, mob of ignorant *wudjellas*. I'm sick to the gut of their false promises of self-determination. Sick of their shit lies, their corrupt laws, their diseases, their gaols . . . yeah, their chains, their chains. They handcuffed me, my *murras*, to a *wudjella* cop. The bastards . . . a *wudjella* pig.

RUBY: I never hear you talk like this, with so much anger. You grow like man now. Your father be real proud if he see you now. But you don't use your *murras* for the things you were taught. You do carving still, Wilba? Make boomerang, spear, emu eggs? What your father think of that if — ?

WILBA: [*interrupting*] He's dead! Mum, you not listening to me. They are going to dig up his bones to build a mining town. That's what this is all about. I can't do those things here, not in the city. We have to fight so that our traditional people can still do these things and keep their land.

RUBY: Alright, but just look after yourself. Don't worry about me, I'll be alright.

WILBA: Mum, I'll be okay, there's big mob of us.

[*A car horn sounds, off.*]

That's my lift. Mum, I gotta do this — for you, for Dad, for me. We've always been told what to do, where to live, where to go. Manipulated like cattle, just like Granny said, but you know them *wudjellas* from government, they decide what we want, what we need, where the money should be spent, but our people are still dying.

RUBY: You know what you talking about, I don't understand. I'll be here when you get back.

[*The car horn sounds again, off.*]

WILBA: That's it. Sorry, Mum, I don't want to sound too heavy, but this is what's happening. There's a lot of angry blacks out there, and I'm one of them. We are all victims of this system, but we are going to do something about it. Mum, I gotta go, and if you see Jayda, say hello for me, aye?

[WILBA *lifts* RUBY *to her feet and puts his arms around her.*]

I'll drop you a line, and don't worry. Come here, I love you. I'll think of you, okay? See ya, see ya . . .

[WILBA *kisses* RUBY *and exits.* RUBY *looks at the door as he closes it, then slowly walks back to the sofa. She gazes around the room fixing her eyes on the artifacts that her family has made. She reminisces about her life as she gathers each piece and places it beside Charlie's totem. She stares fixedly at the totem for a long time.*]

RUBY: Charlie, I seen too many changes. Moon, water, seagrass, dugong, parrotfish . . . all scattered. Granny gone. Wilba's *murras* are scarred by the *wudjella*'s chains. His *murras* are clenched fists now. Jayda don't make baskets no more. She bleeds from her womb the seeds of death. She carries the scars from the *wudjella*'s medicine. There's no place for baskets here, she says. And my *murras* are too weak. They no longer carve. They are empty now. Moon, water, seagrass, dugong, parrotfish . . . gone. All gone.

[*The song 'Visions' plays while the cast slowly move the props off-stage. The* MIMI SPIRIT *dances around the stage until he completes a full circle.*]

THE END

GLOSSARY

The Aboriginal words used in *Murras* are from the Ngarrenjeri and Pitjantjatjara languages.

MURRAS, hands
BOOGADIES, shoes
GUNDIES, underwear
NUNGARS, Aboriginal people
GADJERI, Aboriginal Woman (friend)
WUDJELLAS, white people (non-Aboriginal)
DOOLUM, head lice
INMA, special ceremony, dance
DIDJERIDU, musical instrument (traditional)
CURLEW, bird (when heard the call of this bird means death)

COORDAH

Above: Michael Fuller Snr. as Treb, Mingli Wanjurri as Elly.
Below: Justine Saunders as Tara, Trevor Parfitt as Ginna. Western
Australian Theatre Company production. Photos: Gerhard
Freudenthaller.

Laura Black as Jun
Photo: Gerhard Freudenthaller.

Franklyn Nannup as Nummy. W.A.T.C. production. Photo:
Gerhard Freudenthaller.

Coordah was first performed by the Western Australian Theatre Company at the Hayman Theatre, Curtin University, Perth, on 24 September, 1987 with the following cast:

ELLY	Mingli Wanjurri
TREB	Michael Fuller (Snr)
GINNA	Trevor Parfitt
NUMMY	Franklyn Nannup
SARGE/BROTHER	
DAVIS/GENE	Phil Thomson
TARA	Justine Saunders
JUNE	Laura Black
GAZ	Shane Abdullah
TANK	Joe Walley
KOOLBARDI	Richard Walley
JILLAWARA	Athol Hansen
NURSE	Laura Black

Directed by Richard Walley
Designed by Richard Walley/Steve Nolan
Lighting designed by Duncan Ord

CHARACTERS

TREB, a father figure in his early fifties

ELLY, Treb's wife, in her forties

GINNA, a mentally retarded man, mid-twenties

NUMMY, an inveterate liar and alcoholic, late thirties

SARGE, a white policeman, early forties

TARA, an attractive woman, early thirties

BROTHER DAVIS, white minister of religion, June's father, early fifties

JUNE, a journalist, early twenties

GAZ

TANK   Nummy's mates

KOOLBARDI, a half-caste man, mid-twenties

JILLAWARRA, a man in his mid-twenties

NURSE, a white woman, mid-twenties

GENE, a conservative political candidate, mid-thirties

SETTING

A small country town, with the play spanning the period from 1940 to the present.

ACT ONE

SCENE ONE

The kitchen, morning. TREB *and* ELLY *are alone.* ELLY *opens the fridge and looks for a while, then turns to* TREB.

ELLY: Where did all this meat come from?

TREB: The boys got it last night. They pinched a sheep from Fold's place.

ELLY: How many times I gotta tell you blokes about bringing stolen stuff into this house?

TREB: Not you blokes — them blokes.

ELLY: Don't play innocent with me. How did they get out to Fold's?

TREB: I drove 'em out. They said they were going to buy one.

ELLY: But on the way out youse decided to steal one and save the money for drink.

TREB: Yeh. How did you know?

ELLY: It's not the first time.

[ELLY *looks at a box on the floor and opens it up, then looks at* TREB *again.*]

What these chooks doing here?

TREB: What chooks?

ELLY: These chooks!

[*She picks one out of the box.*]

TREB: Oh . . . they're Nummy's. Huh, he couldn't catch a sheep and the boys were teasing him, so while we were skinning it, Nummy walked over to Scott's and stole them chooks — and the box, too. And Tank was so drunk, he couldn't even catch a chook. So he stole the vegies.

ELLY: What vegies?

TREB: In the cupboard.

[ELLY *walks toward the cupboard but stops when she hears a knock on the door.*]

It's probably Uncle Blue looking for the boys.

[ELLY *looks through the crack of the door and shouts to* TREB.]

ELLY: Moonarch!

[*She opens the door. Sergeant enters.*]

Hello, Sarge.

SARGE: Hello, Eileen. Is Nummy home? We want to have a word with him.

ELLY: I'll see if he's awake. He's been a bit sick lately. He went to bed early last night.

[ELLY *exits into the back room. Meanwhile* TREB *walks to the door.*]

TREB: How ya going, Sarge?

SARGE: Morning, Treb — how you keeping?

TREB: Oh, still hanging. What's he been up to now?

SARGE: We're investigating the disappearance of a sheep from Fold's property and we're hoping Nummy could help us with our enquiries.

TREB: Why an investigation over one sheep?

SARGE: The sheep is a prize ram worth thirty-five thousand dollars!

TREB: Boy! That's expensive lamb chops!

SARGE: We're hoping to either find the sheep or the person or persons who took it before Fold does. He reckons he's gunna kill 'em . . . and seeing that Nummy is the local sheep expert, so to speak, we thought we'd start with him.

ELLY: Sorry, Sarge — he's already gone.

SARGE: Will you tell him we would like to see him down at the station? Thanks, Elly.

ELLY: Sure, Sarge.

[ELLY *shuts the door and punches* TREB.]

SCENE TWO

Blackness. A telephone rings. A man in his mid thirties is lit up answering the phone. The man is GENE, *a worker for a political party.*

GENE: Hello. Oh, how you going, sir? Yes, this is Gene. Oh, I am okay. What do you mean I sound a bit sick? No, I am in perfect health. Yes. What kind of a job? That's up in the north — way up. But sir, how do you campaign among abos? You can't get them to vote — let alone vote for our party! Use my initiative. . . . OK sir, I'll give it a go. Yeh, bye. Abos voting.

[*The light fades.*]

SCENE THREE

Lights come up on two Aborigines sharing a bottle next to a log amid bush. One of the men is NUMMY, *known as the local drunk. The other is mentally retarded. He is* GINNA.

GINNA: But Elly said I not to drink.

NUMMY: Sip it. You're not drinking then — just sipping.

GINNA: Yeh — and den what you done?

NUMMY: Well, after about a hour I said to them *wetjalas*, 'Put your guns away. I'll show youse how to catch a 'roo'. None of them white fellas knew how to shoot! Anyway, they laughed at me and said 'OK, smart arse — show us what you can do!' So I picked up two stones and walked toward the creek and they followed me. At the bottom of the creek was this big boomer. Must have been about, or between five or seven feet tall.

GINNA: And you killed him?

NUMMY: No. He was too big. Them big ones no good — too tough. No. I stayed behind the bush and told the *wetjalas* to be still and quiet . . . then soon, a smaller one hopped along. When he reached the water . . .

GINNA: You shot him.

NUMMY: No. I just whistled and the 'roos stood up looking around. Then I threw one of the stones, high up in the air and they looked up watching it. They didn't want it to land on their head. Then I threw the other stone and hit the 'roo fair in the head — killing him stone dead.

GINNA: The big one.

NUMMY: No, the middle-sized one.

GINNA: What middle-size one?

NUMMY: Oh, he hopped in when the stone was in the air and looked up.

GINNA: You musta thrown the stone a long way up.

NUMMY: Yeh. I hit a duck too. It was flying past at the same time.

[NUMMY's *story is interrupted by* TREB, *who enters carrying a guitar.* TREB *is* NUMMY's *brother-in-law and* GINNA's *brother.*]

TREB: What are you two up to?

GINNA: Hey, my brother.

NUMMY: Treb. We just yarning.

GINNA: Yeh, boy. Just yarning.

TREB: You blokes not drinking?

NUMMY: No.

GINNA: No. We just sipping.

TREB: Ginna. You know Elly will flog you if you go home with just a smell of drink on you!

[GINNA *bows his head.*]

Did you save me a charge?

[NUMMY *hands* TREB *the bottle. He takes a drink and shakes his head.*]

Where did you get this *gebba* from?

NUMMY: It's home made — old Tony. Only eighty cents a bottle.

TREB: Phoo! It's rotten stuff!

[*He drinks some more.*]

NUMMY: Well. Let's do some real rehearsing.

[NUMMY *pulls out another bottle as* TREB *strums his old guitar.* GINNA *just smiles.*]

SCENE FOUR

The lights come up on GENE *as he looks around. He is met by* TREB, NUMMY *and* GINNA, *all talking and none listening.*

GENE: Excuse me! Excuse me, fellows.

NUMMY: Us?

GENE: Yes. I was wondering if I could have a word with youse.

NUMMY: You a cop?

GENE: No.

NUMMY: From the Aboriginal Department?

GENE: No.

NUMMY: You own a pub?

GENE: No, I am —

NUMMY: [*interrupting*] Well you're talking to the wrong blokes.

> [*The three walk away, leaving* GENE *trying to reason with their departing backs.*]

GENE: I am here to try to help you. I am from . . .

> [*He wanders off.* NUMMY *turns to the others.*]

NUMMY: I went to a meeting last week and I got up to have my say and the Chairman told me to sit down. He said I must speak through the Chair, so I sat down, then I grabbed the chair in front of me, lifted it up and spoke through it! And I said to them 'Now I'm gonna have *my* say.'

> [*The lights fade.*]

SCENE FIVE

Preacher BROTHER DAVIS *talks to his daughter.*

DAVIS: The indigents of this country are a fascinating people: they are very proud, yet humble. They are very savage, yet gentle. They have fights, yet there is a strong bond between them; they are very Christian, more sincere and trusting than us, us so called civilized people, yet they still practise the old paganistic ways.

JUNE: And that's the part that really bothers you, doesn't it?

DAVIS: You can't believe in Jesus on Sundays, then practise rituals through the week; it's just not right.

JUNE: Christians have been doing that for years, father.

DAVIS: Not Christians, my dear, just people who don't really want to believe in Jesus. . . but they want some sort of insurance in case there is a — in their prevaricating minds, heaven; and more significantly, no one wants to go to hell.

JUNE: Why do you stay here? How long has it been now . . .? Sixteen years?

DAVIS: Eighteen years.

JUNE: Eighteen years; you spent — what? Two or three years in India, another two or three in South America, another one or two in New Guinea —

DAVIS: [*interrupting*] Don't forget Africa.

JUNE: Why? Why eighteen years here . . .?

DAVIS: You'll know, after being here for a while . . . you'll know . . .

JUNE: I am only going to be here for two weeks.

DAVIS: That's long enough . . .

JUNE: You're not feeling guilty about dragging Mum all over the world, 'till . . .

DAVIS: It's got nothing to do with guilt. I feel no guilt for what happened. We discussed everything. There was no guarantee that the native remedy would have worked anyway.

JUNE: Sorry . . . I am sorry, Dad . . . I guess being a journalist gives me a cynical look at people and situations. If I was a man I would be an editor by now. My stories were the truth, fixed up with a bit of journalistic licence to stress a point.

DAVIS: The world is not ready for ya, yet.

JUNE: This is the forties for . . . heck sake father . . . Women should be treated with the respect they command when they achieve . . . Who's that?

DAVIS: Who's where?

JUNE: Over there . . . those two.

DAVIS: Which one do you want to know about?

JUNE: The fair-skinned one . . . He's not a native is he?

DAVIS: He, my dear, is *Koolbardi* . . . a half-caste . . . caught between two worlds. His grandfather is one of the old lawkeepers; wants him to learn and keep the practice going, but Jillawarra, another trainee lawkeeper, says his mind has been poisoned by us *wetjalas*.

JUNE: How?

DAVIS: He was sent to school . . . gained an education. His mother wanted him to learn about *wetjala*'s world.

JUNE: Wise woman.

DAVIS: The evenings are beautiful here . . . You could smell the aroma of the gum trees in the breeze.

JUNE: I could write a good story on that.

DAVIS: Evenings?

JUNE: No, the half-caste human interest story . . . half tame . . . half savage.

DAVIS: Let me tell you something and listen good. I'll only tell you this once. Don't mess with these people: they are not guinea pigs for you or any anthropologist to research and document to satisfy your curiosity.

JUNE: Your own private stock, eh?

DAVIS: They are no one's stock, you hear me? No one's stock . . . Good night . . . God bless.

SCENE SIX

KOOLBARDI *and* JILLAWARRA *talk,* JILLAWARRA *in his language.*

JILLAWARRA: You wrong!

KOOLBARDI: No . . . I am not . . . and you know I'm not. I tell you it's —

JILLAWARRA: [*interrupting*] You tell, you tell, you always tell . . . Do you ever listen?

KOOLBARDI: Yes, I listen . . . I listen to both sides of all stories, then I weigh both sides and I then know which side is right.

JILLAWARRA: There is only one true way.

KOOLBARDI: That depends on what you want to believe. If you want to believe . . . you could make anything true.

JILLAWARRA: No, you can't. The law was made in the Dreamtime, when everything was true . . . Then Carda, he made the poison . . . He wanted to rule the land . . . he thought he was the smartest, but he was tricked by the snake . . . the

most harmless fella . . . then Snake thought he was great
'cause he had the poison, but look what happened to him!

KOOLBARDI: Yer, but they only stories.

JILLAWARRA: I knew one day you gunna say that . . . I knew it
. . . you gone all white, *wetjala* make you *kartworra*.

KOOLBARDI: I don't know why I talk to you . . . You'll never
understand what I am on about.

JILLAWARRA: True . . . I'll never understand you or what
you're on about . . . you know we are all one . . . us, the
animals, the plants, the rocks, the land . . . we are all one.

KOOLBARDI: True . . . some blokes have rocks in their head,
dirt on their face and are real animals.

JILLAWARRA: That's not funny.

KOOLBARDI: I am only joking.

JILLAWARRA: It's no joking matter. You wanna watch yourself.

KOOLBARDI: Listen . . . can't we go through one day without
arguing?

JILLAWARRA: We could if you wasn't so bloody pigheaded!

KOOLBARDI: I am not pigheaded . . . you're the bloke.

JILLAWARRA: Hey, look here.

[*Jillawarra points to ground.*]

KOOLBARDI: What?

JILLAWARRA: Shoo-i . . . be quiet . . . stay close behind me.

KOOLBARDI: What is it?

JILLAWARRA: Shoo-i.

[*He motions to* KOOLBARDI *to get behind him.* JILLAWARRA
reaches under a rock and pulls out a snake.]

He is a beauty, eh? Here, hold it for me.

KOOLBARDI: Don't mess around, Jilla . . . I'll kill you.

[JILLAWARRA *chases* KOOLBARDI *off stage.*]

SCENE SEVEN

TREB *and* ELLY'*s place.* GINNA *lies asleep on the lounge.* TREB *and* NUMMY *enter, arguing.*

TREB: How many times I gotta tell you? When I nod my head you stop.

NUMMY: But you nod your head all the way through from start to bloody finish.

TREB: Don't you know the difference between rhythm movements and nodding, you bloody idiot?

NUMMY: Not with your head! You ought to get your neck tightened up.

[ELLY *and* TARA *walk in carrying shopping bags as* NUMMY *and* TREB *sit down.*]

ELLY: How did practice go?

TREB: Rehearsals, love. I did good but them other blokes need months. They're fucken hopeless, true!

NUMMY: Hey! I was good.

TREB: Yeh, but then you started playing . . . Ha, ha . . .

NUMMY: I bet you have to hold this bloke's head still when you have to do something stupid — like kiss him.

[NUMMY *notices* TARA.]

Hey, Tara baby.

TARA: I'm not your baby.

NUMMY: You know you always come over here to see me. Give me a kiss.

TARA: Piss off — you stupid jerk.

NUMMY: Arr . . . You say that so lovely.

ELLY: Nummy, behave yourself.

TREB: Let him be. You could see they were made for each other.

TARA: Don't you start or I'll tell Eileen about you and that Chinese girl — Rosie . . . what's her name?

TREB: Rosie who?

TARA: Yeh, that's her. Rosie Hoo.

ELLY: And you told me you were going to practise.

TREB: Honest, love. Nummy, tell her where we was.

NUMMY: What's this '*we*'? I don't know where *you* was.

TREB: Hey, I just took it up for you.

ELLY: We're only teasing, no need to get wild.

TREB: Yeh, and if you wasn't teasing, would you believe this liar?

NUMMY: I don't tell lies. Search me.

ELLY: Who wants a drink?

TREB: You got some?

ELLY: Only one bottle.

TARA: I'll see you fellas later.

NUMMY: Just say — I'll meet you at lovers' lane, eh?

TARA: I wouldn't be seen with you anywhere, twit!

NUMMY: But just say.

ELLY:
TREB: [*together*] See you, sis.

NUMMY: Gee, that woman is so mad about me.

[ELLY *notices* GINNA *asleep on the lounge.*]

ELLY: Has he been drinking?

TREB: Not with me. You know I've been to work. Then after work we were rehearsing, then came straight home.

NUMMY: Sister, you know I wouldn't let him drink.

[GINNA *rolls and falls off the lounge.*]

GINNA: Oh, shit!

ELLY: You all right, Ginna? You okay?

GINNA: Hey, my sister-in-law! I love you. As God is my witness, I love you. I love my big brother Treb . . . and my little sister Tara . . . and most I love my *coordah*, Nummy.

ELLY: You been drinking?

[GINNA *looks to* NUMMY, *who shakes his head.*]

GINNA: No, just sipping. Me and Nummy just been sipping.

ELLY: Nummy, you bloody liar, how many times I told you? You know he's got a plate in his head. One drunken fall could kill him. He is a sick man.

NUMMY: He as tough as a leather boot — and smarter than you fellas think he is.

[ELLY *hits* NUMMY *with a boot, knocking him off his chair, then takes* GINNA *by the arm.*]

ELLY: (*to* NUMMY) I don't want to hear any more from you. Ginna, you're going to bed.

[ELLY *takes* GINNA *through one door, then reappears, goes into her own bedroom and slams the door.*]

TREB: See: you got me into shit again.

NUMMY: That shouldn't worry you, you so full of it.

TREB: Don't start or I'll knock your fucken head off. Just two more words out of you and down you go.

NUMMY: But . . .

TREB: That's one.

[NUMMY *grabs the bottle. Blackout.*]

SCENE EIGHT

TREB *and* ELLY's *place, a little later.* TREB *and* NUMMY *talk animatedly.*

TREB: I'll open up by making a speech about how we got started in this business.

NUMMY: What business?

TREB: You know: the pioneers — now the living legends of traditional country music.

NUMMY: But no one knows us.

TREB: Yeh, but these fellas won't know that. We'll tell 'em we were on the country music show.

NUMMY: *Look.* Everyone knows us around here — they'll know it's all lies.

TREB: Make up your mind! First you say no one knows us — then you say everyone knows us. What are you . . . a fucken idiot?

NUMMY: I meant . . . no one knows us as musicians.

[*The argument is interrupted by a knock on the door.* NUMMY *hides the bottle.*]

TREB: Who's there?

[*Two boys enter the room:* GAZ *and* TANK.]

GAZ: What we gunna do?

TREB: What we gunna do about what?

TANK: Rehearsals.

TREB: What fucken rehearsals?

GAZ: Rehearsals for the ball.

TREB: What have you blokes got to do with the ball?

TANK: You said we all gunna dance together, remember?

TREB: When? None of you bastards can dance: youse can't stay sober long enough to learn.

TANK: But you said Nummy will show us if we come around next week and bring a few bottles.

TREB: But Nummy's up . . . or . . . yeh, now. Remember. Yeh, Nummy's solid.

NUMMY: I am?

TREB: Yeh. Did youse bring the bottles?

GAZ: Yeh. We only brought a couple of cartons.

TREB: Bring 'em in, then. We'll rehearse later on.

NUMMY: But I can't dance . . .

TREB: When you're sober, eh? That's what you mean. Oh, you can't teach while you're sober. Old law, eh?

TANK: You know, we was all talk when we was drunk. But when we sobered up, we had another talk among ourselves, you know . . . and I said to the Gaz that bloody Treb is right, we should be proud of our culture . . . and we should take advantage of Nummy's experience. Not too many people danced for the Prime Minister, the Queen, the Pope and Charlie Pride. They is important people.

GAZ: Yeh — and playing the didgeridoo at the same time.

TANK: And youse also gunna teach Aboriginal song, eh?

NUMMY: But I never danced or played —

TREB: [*interrupting*] For your own people before, eh? Where them bottles, Gaz?

TANK: Get the bottles. We'll celebrate the revival of our precious culture.

NUMMY: Yeh — and the cutting short of my precious life!

[*Blackout.*]

SCENE NINE

TREB *and* ELLY's *place later still. Bodies lie everywhere.* TREB *and* NUMMY *are still sitting up, each with a bottle in hand.*

NUMMY: Yeh, brother: I'll show them how to *nyumbi*. We'll have a good dance group by the time I finish with them.

TREB: I'll have to show you how to *nyumbi* first.

NUMMY: You reckon I can't dance?

TREB: I don't reckon — I know you can't dance.

NUMMY: Well what you go tell them lies for?

TREB: Lies? I never told them lies. Listen, when we got drunk last time you was tapping your foot in time to a Charlie Pride song, the Pope was on the newspaper in front of you and the Prime Minister was talking to the Queen on TV.

NUMMY: But I can *nyumbi*, you know. I am good at it; when we were kids we used to go with old Nyubri and he used to teach us a lot of things.

TREB: Like drinking, smoking, swearing, telling lies —

NUMMY: [*interrupting*] Don't make fun of old Nyubri — he was a solid old bloke. He really did show us a lot.

TREB: Well, you better remember the dancing parts quick or I'll have to tell Tank you told me lies.

NUMMY: I'll knock your bloody head off if you start!

TREB: If I start what, eh? If I start what? I'll put you fair on your arse, you try to be smart with me.

NUMMY: Sleep is the smartest thing you do. That way you're not giving anyone the shits.

TREB: I knock the shit out of you, you keep going.

NUMMY: You're okay in your own place — but we can't keep you locked up in the shithouse all day. Other people have to use it.

TREB: Don't push your luck, you jerk.

NUMMY: You pull your luck, don't you?

TREB: That's it! I've had enough of you — you flamin' twit.

NUMMY: I've had enough of you too, turkey.

TREB: I want you out of the house in the morning — for real
   this time, too. No sweet talk about being drunk either —
   'cause I'm sober now when I say this.
NUMMY: I'll get out of here and don't ask me to stop, too —
   'cause I had a gut full of you.
   [ELLY *enters and looks around the room.*]
ELLY: What's been going on here?
TREB: 'Ello lub! You 'wake, eh?
ELLY: What these blokes doing here? What's going on?
NUMMY: They all my pupils, sis.
ELLY: What? You teaching them to be alc'holics or idiots?
TREB: Ha! Good one, Mum!
ELLY: Don't you 'Good one, Mum' me, you. And don't you
   think about coming to bed in that state.
NUMMY: Leave the mongrel, sis, shift out with me in the
   morning after I punch his lights out.
TREB: Huh! You don't get up till the afternoon — but I'll have
   you up bright and early to get you out of here.
ELLY: You moving out again?
NUMMY: Yes, sis.
ELLY: That'll be five times in the last fortnight. You betta shut
   up — it's five in the morning — other people want to sleep,
   even if you don't.

SCENE TEN

KOOLBARDI *sits outside and looks at the stars.* JUNE *approaches.*

JUNE: Beautiful, aren't they?
KOOLBARDI: What?
JUNE: The stars. They're beautiful.
KOOLBARDI: Sure are.
JUNE: I'm June. You're Koolbardi, ain't you?
KOOLBARDI: Yeh. But you can call me Peter.
JUNE: Peter.

KOOLBARDI: Yeh, Peter. Named after the fellow in the Bible. You see, us *nyoongahs* never had two names — so I was called Peter Koolbardi.

JUNE: Do you know who I am?

KOOLBARDI: Yeh, the whole tribe know. No secrets around here.

JUNE: Why won't youse talk to me?

KOOLBARDI: You have to earn trust around here.

JUNE: How do I do that?

KOOLBARDI: I don't know. Never figured that one out.

JUNE: You're not afraid to talk, though.

KOOLBARDI: I have spent time with white fellas — went to their school. My father was a white fella.

JUNE: Must be hard for you, you know, caught between two worlds. Is there really much difference between us?

KOOLBARDI: Well . . .

JUNE: Tell me about your lifestyle.

KOOLBARDI: Nothing to tell. We sleep, wake, eat, breathe — you know — all those boring natural things.

JUNE: What about your dances? What dances do you do?

KOOLBARDI: I do a couple. I learnt a new one last year: the barn dance.

JUNE: Not our dances! Your traditional dances.

KOOLBARDI: What about them?

JUNE: Can you tell me about them?

KOOLBARDI: Some. Some I can . . . but not all of them.

JUNE: Why can't you tell me?

KOOLBARDI: You want to know whitefellas' biggest problem? They always ask *why*. Everything is 'Why'. 'Why do you do this?' 'Why is that there?' 'Why do you eat?' Never accept anything — always 'Why?'

JUNE: Well, what's wrong with that?

KOOLBARDI: Second biggest problem, ' *What*'. 'What is that?' 'What do you do?' '*What*?'

JUNE: Okay . . . no more questions. I just wanted to know more about you.

KOOLBARDI: Oh, I could have told you. I am single, smart single. Good hunter . . . dancer . . . musician . . . storyteller . . . horse rider . . . and single.

JUNE: Then I take it you're not married.

KOOLBARDI: Gee, you're bloody quick.

JUNE: Are youse carniverous?

KOOLBARDI: No, mostly Anglican.

JUNE: No — I mean you . . . youse . . .

KOOLBARDI: Whitefellas' third most asked word: 'Are youse this?' . . . 'Are youse that?'

JUNE: Sorry. No more questions. It's a silly habit that I have.

KOOLBARDI: Got any more?

JUNE: What?

KOOLBARDI: Silly habits.

JUNE: Why?

KOOLBARDI: Your last two words were what and why.

　　　[*Fade to black.*]

SCENE ELEVEN

TREB *and* ELLY's *place, next morning.* TREB *is up;* NUMMY *sleeps at the table,* TANK *on the lounge chair,* GAZ *on the floor.*

TREB: [*to* NUMMY] Hey *coordah*! Cup of tea here!

NUMMY: Oh, my head, What's today?

TREB: Friday morning. Betta clean up before Elly wakes.

NUMMY: Yeh. I'll help you drekley. Hey, these blokes still here! Hey, you blokes — Gaz, Tank. Get up. Youse want a cup of tea? Treb got a big fire going outside. He cooking our catch.

　　　[*On the lounge chair* TANK *starts to stir, which develops into a frenzy when he finds his hand caught in the upholstery.*]

TANK: Let me go! Let me go you mongrel bastard! I'm not going! Let my hand go!

　　　[*As* TANK *comes to his senses he looks around at everyone.*]

TREB: Your hand is stuck in the spring.

TANK: I was having a bloody nightmare!

TREB: You sure was!

TANK: I was dreaming that a pure gold ball about this big rolled into a hole — so I put my hand in to get it — and the devil was waiting for me. Then he grabbed me and was trying to pull me to hell.

TREB: Nummy's been fixing that chair for the last six months.

GAZ: Yeh, thanks. What happened last night?

TREB: You blokes danced your feet off. You fellas solid, boy. You must be hungry now.

GAZ: Yeh. I am, alright.

TREB: You blokes will be deadly at the ball.

GAZ: But I think we'll need another practice before Monday. You know, to refreshen our memory.

TREB: Don't worry! Nummy will show youse again. Come on, now . . . let's have a feed.

[*The boys exit with* TREB. NUMMY *stays in the room. He is soon joined by* ELLY.]

ELLY: Pooh, this place stinks.

NUMMY: Hey, never took my shoes off.

ELLY: Where's everyone?

NUMMY: At the back.

ELLY: Tara will be here soon to pick me up.

NUMMY: Where you two going?

ELLY: Shopping. We gunna throw a surprise party for Treb tonight. It's his birthday on Monday, so we thought we'd throw a small party here for him early. Tell Tank and Gaz to come back at eight or nine if they do leave — but don't let Treb know. I'm going to have my shower now.

NUMMY: I won't let him know anything. I'll even give him ten dollars to go and spend the night at Uncle Blue's.

ELLY: You've got no money.

NUMMY: How do you know?

ELLY: 'Cause it's two days after your social pay.

NUMMY: True . . .

(ELLY *exits.* NUMMY *looks around, then starts to tap his foot. He tries to step in rhythm.* TARA *enters and watches him for a while.*]

TARA: Hey, Fred Astaire! Where's Elly?

NUMMY: She's in the shower. Where you come from? Don't you know how to knock?

TARA: Not when it's open. What you doing? Trying to get a one-way ticket to the funny farm?

NUMMY: I was practising my steps. I'll be teaching the boys how to corroboree for the ball.

TARA: Huh! What is it — a comedy sketch? Nummy and the numbskulls?

NUMMY: You can laugh all you like. You just wait till Monday night. You'll be stunned and you'll fall madly in love with me.

TARA: Who'd want to fall for a twit like you?

NUMMY: You know you secretly love me.

TARA: If murder was legal I'd kill you every day of the week. Have you seen a blue ear ring around? I lost one last time I was here.

NUMMY: Yeh. It was on the lounge chair — and it fell in the ripped part.

[TARA *puts her hand into the rip; she finds nothing but gets her hand stuck.*]

TARA: Nummy! Help me! My hand is stuck.

NUMMY: You mean stuck stuck?

TARA: Yeh, stuck stuck — you dope.

[NUMMY *walks behind* TARA.]

What are you doing?

[NUMMY *squeezes* TARA's *bum,* TARA *yeecks.*]

Don't mess around, you stupid. Don't Nummy — I'm gunna kill you.

[NUMMY *keeps fondling* TARA, *then suddenly runs to the door as* EILEEN *emerges and walks toward* TARA.]

Help me out of here. I'm going to kill that Nummy!

NUMMY: See you, sis. See you love.

[NUMMY *runs out the door.*]

ELLY: Been here long?

TARA: Too bloody long.

TREB *and* ELLY'*s place, night. The lights are out. The door opens and* TREB *storms in.*

TREB: Nummy, I'm gunna kill you, you lying bastard. There's no one at Uncle Blue's. I walked all the way over there, got chased by that fucken dog — all for nothing. Where the fucken light? Nummy . . . you bastard . . . a man spend a hard day working — then sent on a wild goose chase!

[*The lights are switched on to reveal* ELLY, TANK, GAZ, NUMMY *and* TARA.]

OTHERS: Surprise!

ELLY: An early happy birthday, darling.

TREB: My birthday is not till Monday.

ELLY: You wouldn't have been surprised if we had it Monday.

TANK: Happy birthday, cuz.

GAZ: Happy birthday, Treb.

NUMMY: Happy fifty-sixth, *coordah.*

TREB: That's what you two were up to!

[TREB *and* ELLY *stand around the table and talk.* NUMMY *and the boys go to the other side of the room.*]

NUMMY: You know, if you play with yourself, very fine white hair grows on your hand.

[GAZ *and* TANK *look at their hands.*]

Yeh, fellas. I want it kept very quiet but Tara and me will be getting engaged soon. She wanted to announce it tonight, but I told her to wait a while. This is Treb's party, not ours. The poor girl is so anxious to tell everyone — she's really mad about me.

TANK: I find that hard to understand.

NUMMY: Yeh, but you find everything hard to understand.

TANK: What do you mean by that?

NUMMY: Need I say more?

GAZ: You mean you'll be our cousin two ways?

NUMMY: I'm not your cousin any way.

GAZ: I mean in law — you know — Treb and Tara are our cousins.

NUMMY: Oh, yeh.

TANK: [*loudly*] But what do you mean, I don't understand. All I was trying to understand was what a smart girl like Tara sees in a nut like you — to talk you into marrying her.

> [TARA *overhears the conversation, rushes across and hits* NUMMY *with her bag.*]

TARA: What going on here?

NUMMY: Arr love — don't play up in front of the boys.

GAZ: Congratulations, cuz!

TARA: Don't you 'Congratulations, cuz' me. Don't believe anything this bloody idiot tells you. He's a twit. You tell yarns about me in any way associated with you, I'll kill you. You got that?

NUMMY: Yes, lub — I mean yes, yes.

TREB: Isn't love beautiful?

ELLY: Don't you start.

TANK: But what did you mean, 'wouldn't understand' . . . ?

GAZ: When we gunna practise, Nummy?

NUMMY: Let's go to the stump and practise tomorrow night. I'll grab my old didgeridoo and music sticks.

TREB: You sold them last week.

NUMMY: I did not sell them! Just borrowed on them. Old Jonesy said I can use them anytime I want them.

TANK: I really am proud to be with you, Nummy. For the first time in my life I can see the culture in you . . . and for me to be a part of it really made me have another look at myself. I am not gunna drink anymore till we finished our bit at the ball next week.

GAZ: That goes for me too.

TANK: I really feel good abot this, you know.

> [*The lights fade.*]

SCENE THIRTEEN

The bush meeting place. NUMMY *walks in, followed by* TANK, *then* TREB, GAZ *and* GINNA. NUMMY *stops, looks around, then directs the rest of them where they should sit.*

NUMMY: Tank, you sit there, you there Gaz, you two over there.

> [NUMMY *sits the fellas down in a circle. He realises there is no place for him. They reorganise to give him room.*]

Now I'll show youse how to corroboree one at a time. I'll show you the moves and you have to practise yourself.

> [NUMMY *shows the dancers one at a time. The lights fade.*]

SCENE FOURTEEN

The same, some time later. NUMMY, TANK, GAZ, TREB *and* GINNA *look tired.*

NUMMY: Look, we been practising for hours now and you still haven't got it.

TANK: We still got Saturday and Sunday night to practise.

TREB: Let's not stay here too long — it's two o'clock in the morning by now.

NUMMY: That's the best time: all the spirits will be out.

GAZ: What spirits?

NUMMY: All the spirits. The good spirits and the evil ones.

GINNA: What do they do?

TREB: Just suck your blood out of you.

NUMMY: Poor spirit will be drunk if it sucked the blood out of you blokes!

TANK: It's not funny! They can hear you talk, you know.

NUMMY: They don't like blokes talking loud, either.

GAZ: Why?

GINNA: Don't ask.

TREB: Noise travels in waves, and it —
GAZ: [*interrupting*] I'll scream at the bastards if they come near
    me.
    [*The lights fade.*]

SCENE FIFTEEN

TREB *and* ELLY's *place, morning.* ELLY *hands* TREB *a cup of tea.*

TREB: Thanks love. Nummy and Ginna up yet?
ELLY: Yeh. They went over to Uncle Blue's — the boys are
    practising or rehearsing — or whatever youse do.
TREB: What? This time of the day? What time is it now?
ELLY: It's about nine o'clock. Nummy left at seven.
    [TARA *enters.*]
TARA: Morning.
ELLY: Morning.
TREB: Gooday.
TARA: What's the boys up to? They're all over Uncle Blue's
    place locked in the shed — and there's a lot of noise coming
    from it.
ELLY: They're all practising a corroboree that Nummy is
    teaching them.
TARA: Nummy? What's he gunna teach them?
ELLY: Nummy used to dance a lot when he was a young bloke.
    He used to follow old Nyubri around everywhere.
TARA: You know what's so unusual about the whole thing?
ELLY: What?
TARA: They were all sober. Uncle Blue couldn't get over it. He
    hid his bottles when he seen Nummy coming, but he left six
    cans in the fridge. Nummy opened the fridge door, pushed
    the beer aside and had a drink of *milk*. Then he went out to
    the shed where the boys sleep. They locked the door and we
    been wondering what they have been up to.
ELLY: Nummy really pushed the beer aside?
TREB: No. She only joking.

TARA: No joking. It's true.

TREB: I hope they don't go and hurt themselves. They never done anything sober before.

[*A knock is heard on the door.* ELLY *goes and answers it.*]

ELLY: It's Joe Alicks. He wants to see you, Treb.

[TREB *exits to see Joe.*]

I wonder what Joe wants to see Treb for.

TARA: Joe is on the social committee of the race club. He might be telling him what time they want him and Nummy to be on.

ELLY: I bet they deliberately put them on late so they can make fools of themselves again. You know old Treb is a good singer when he's sober — but when he's drunk the words just drag out and Nummy plays, stops, yarns and starts up again. It must be funny to other people.

[TREB *enters.*]

ELLY: What did he want?

TREB: He said that a television camera is gunna be at the ball. Part's going to be televised live around the State. It's to do with the charity appeal so they wanted me to stay sober. I'm going to be the highlight of the night.

ELLY: Oh, that's good.

TARA: That's solid, brother.

[TREB *doesn't look happy.*]

ELLY: We always said you are the best singer and guitar player we've ever seen and heard, eh Tara?

TARA: Yeh. You better stay sober.

ELLY: Oh boy! Wait till I tell everyone. Why the gloom? . . . You should be happy. This is the biggest event of the year for this whole area and you're going to be the highlight — so why no smile?

TREB: They only want me.

ELLY: What do you mean?

TREB: They're bringing entertainers from Perth for the night, so they don't want Nummy to do anything.

ELLY: But he always does something! It's the only thing that keeps him alive from year to year. He talks about what he did last time and what he's going to do next.

[*Pause.*]
   That's all he's got.

TREB: They said he's a nut.

TARA: I won't argue with them . . . Sorry, I shouldn't have said
   that. Who's going to tell him.
      [*Pause.*]
   And the rest of them?

ELLY: They can't be serious.
      [*The lights fade.*]

SCENE SIXTEEN

The same, late that day. NUMMY *and* GINNA *enter.*

NUMMY: Who's home? Anyone in?
      [TREB *enters.*]

TREB: Don't make too much noise. Elly's asleep. What you
   been up to?

NUMMY: We been up to rehearsing. You wanna see the boys
   now. They real solid. We gunna have a big rehearsal
   tomorrow night at the stump — and you know what?
   You're the bloke who started all this. I want to thank you
   from my heart. But we've got a surprise for you. You'll have
   to wait for it though.

TREB: I've a surprise for you, too.

NUMMY: What?

TREB: Nothin.
      [ELLY *walks through bedroom.*]

NUMMY: I'm hitting the sack. I'm cruel tired. Goodnight.
      [NUMMY *exits to his room.*]

TREB: Good night, *coordah.*
      [ELLY *enters.*]

ELLY: Come to bed — it's late. Did Nummy come back yet?
   Did you tell him?

TREB: No. I'll tell him tomorrow.

ELLY: Come to bed.
      [*The lights fade.*]

SCENE SEVENTEEN

TREB *and* ELLY*'s place, Sunday morning.* NUMMY *and* GINNA *are up and about.* NUMMY *knocks on* TREB *and* ELLY*'s door.*

NUMMY: I'll see youse later. The water's boiled and I cooked some pancakes for youse.
> [NUMMY *and* GINNA *exit.* TREB *enters, followed by* ELLY.]
TREB: Nummy, Nummy . . . wait.
ELLY: What's Num doing up so early?
TREB: Probably pissed the bed.
> [ELLY *walks toward the bedroom.*]
I'm only joking. You know why he's up.
ELLY: When you gunna tell him?
TREB: [*angrily*] As soon as I get a bloody chance! [*Controlling himself.*] Sorry, I didn't mean to shout at you. I'm going to see the social committee and tell them to put them on.
> [TREB *hugs* ELLY.]
ELLY: I hope they can do somethin'.
TREB: I'm sure they can.
ELLY: When you gunna see them?
TREB: They meet tonight.
ELLY: Let's go over to Tara's and get her to come with us to the lake for the day. I'll take some damper and kangaroo and we can pick up Uncle Blue and Aunty Flo.
TREB: Don't forget the pancakes.

SCENE EIGHTEEN

The lights come up on GENE *with papers in hand, walking. He is met by* NUMMY *and the boys.*

GENE: Excuse me, fellas.
NUMMY: Why, what have you done?
GENE: Nothing. I want to talk to youse.

NUMMY: Well, you gotta make an appointment. We're pretty busy.

GENE: Who do I make it with?

NUMMY: Ginna. He's our secretary.

GENE: Who's Ginna?

GINNA: Me.

GENE: When can I see youse?

GINNA: Well — you lookin at us now.

GENE: No, I mean talk to youse. You know . . . a yarn. Who's the main man — you know, the spokesman — around here?

GINNA: Arr, my brother, he talks for all of us.

GENE: Could you tell me his name?

GINNA: Yeh.

GENE: Well . . . ?

GINNA: Well, what?

GENE: I asked you, could you tell me his name.

GINNA: Yeh, and I told you I could.

GENE: Well, what is it?

GINNA: 'Treb'. I gotta go now.

GENE: When and where can I catch this Treb?

GINNA: We got a big meeting tomorrow. You might see him there.

GENE: Thanks.

SCENE NINETEEN

Morning, NURSE BURTON'*s office. The* NURSE *writes at her desk.*

NURSE: 'District Manager . . . I have pleasure in submitting this my quarterly report. The Aborigines of this town are coping quite adequately. There is a vast improvement in their health and they are managing their affairs without difficulties . . .'

[TARA *enters.*]

TARA: Morning.

NURSE: Tara, what's it like being an Aboriginal? I mean —
What would you tell me?

[*The* NURSE *continues to write.*]

TARA: Aboriginals will always tell you what you want to know.
That way they get rid of you.

NURSE: What's that?

TARA: Nothing.

NURSE: These last three months have shown me another side
of Aboriginals. You know what I mean.

TARA: That depends on what side you were looking at before.

NURSE: You, for example. You're never late for work or any of
your appointments — you're always clean and tidy, you
don't get drunk — not like the normal Aboriginals.

TARA: I went wrong somewhere.

NURSE: Take for example this meeting I organised for
tomorrow.

TARA: What meeting?

NURSE: You know. The one on sanitation within the house-
hold. [*Turning to the window*] I wouldn't be surprised if only
half a dozen or so turn up. They're not interested in
hygiene. Take for example that last meeting on budgeting
within your means. Eight people turned up and six of them
wanted to borrow money till next pension day!

[TARA *exits quietly as* NURSE BROWN *talks.*]

Then the women's meeting on beauty products by nature.
Remember some of the sales pitches and the tone of voice
that Simone delivered it in . . .

[GENE *enters and looks around.*]

Your hair will be as soft as a rose petal, your skin as smooth
as silk, your eyes will be alluring, your lips inviting, your
breasts uplifting, your buttocks and legs so . . .

[*The* NURSE *notices* GENE.]

Who are you?

GENE: Sorry for walking in — but I did knock.

NURSE: Where's Tara?

GENE: Who?

NURSE: Tara. The girl I was talking to.

GENE: She must have left. Please let me introduce myself. I am Gene Peters. I am campaigning in this area to get Aboriginals to exercise their basic right and vote in the next elections — therefore giving them a say in who represents them in the next parliament.

NURSE: Huh, you're a politician.

GENE: Well, yes.

NURSE: That's all we get around here is politicians . . . apart from anthropologists, medical people and anyone else who wants to study Aborigines. You know this group here must be the most studied group of Aboriginals — no, the most studied group of people — no, the most studied group of anything — in the world. I have been here for three months and I have seen —

GENE: [*interrupting*] You said politicians?

NURSE: Yes, last month. Said he was going to buy the Aborigines tractors, trucks, sheep, cattle and anything else it takes to run their own station and besides.

GENE: What was his name, this politician?

NURSE: Er, 'Mac —' . . . 'Mac —' something or other — 'MacGregons'?

GENE: 'MacGliggens'? 'Robert MacGliggens'?

NURSE: You know him? Anyhow, hope he's no friend of yours. He was told to go. Treb told him. He sounded like a Father Christmas with a bag full of bullshit.

GENE: Who is this Treb character?

NURSE: Treb is Tara's brother. You met Tara, didn't you?

GENE: No, I am sorry.

NURSE: Oh, that's right. She left before you arrived. Anyhow, Treb is sorta the leader around here. He gets people outa jail, talks for them in court, runs them to hospital after a fight or when a woman is about to give birth. He's also a truck driver on the local shire. Been there for years, so I have been told.

GENE: Must be a popular fellow.

NURSE: Yeh. The main reason is that he's the only Aboriginal around here on the phone — and you know the old 'allowed one phone call'! . . . When you got three hundred

Aborigines in the area, that's a lot of phone calls. Well, not really that many: most of them can't use a phone.

GENE: When can I see this Treb?

NURSE: He'll be at . . . oh, no he won't. That's right, Tara said she was going to the lake with them. That's where she went. Anyhow, his phone number is here. Call him later tonight, you can catch him then.

GENE: Thanks. It's been nice talking to you.

NURSE: It's my pleasure. Always glad to have visitors drop by anytime.

SCENE TWENTY

TREB *and* ELLY's *place. They return to the house.*

ELLY: I really enjoyed today.

TREB: Yeh. It was a great day.
  [*The phone rings.*]

ELLY: I'll get it: you put the kettle on.
  [*She picks up the phone.*]
  Hello . . . Yes he is . . . Who's calling? . . . Dean Peters.
  [TREB *takes the phone.*]

TREB: Yeh, well I am pretty busy over the next couple of days . . . Yeah . . . Well, I'm not interested in politics . . . I don't care if you come from the moon . . . No I am not. You're wasting your time mate . . . Well, if no one else will listen to you, what makes you think I will? . . . Oh, so you met Nummy. He a mate of yours? . . . Well, you should be behind bars, pal! Well, listen, if you're a mate of Nummy's, come over and have a cup of tea with us. But don't talk politics . . . Yeh, come straight over. See ya.

ELLY: Who's Dean Peters?

TREB: Gene, not Dean. Ar . . . he reckons he's a mate of Nummy's. Some sort of politician.

ELLY: I don't recall Nummy mentioning his name.

TREB: He didn't, but anyone who claims to be a mate of Nummy's must be desperate.

[*There is a knock on the door.* ELLY *answers and invites* GENE *in.*]

Come on in.

GENE: Thank you. My name is Gene Peters.

ELLY: I am Elly and this is my husband Trevor.

TREB: Pleased to meet you. Any mate of Nummy's is welcome here.

ELLY: Please sit down.

[ELLY *goes to make the tea.*]

GENE: I am not really a mate of Nummy. I don't even know him . . . but I heard he was your brother-in-law and . . .

TREB: We already figured that out, but I listened to that other bloke, MacGliggens, so it's only fair to listen to you.

GENE: Thanks.

TREB: But don't start any bullshit or I'll have to throw you out.

GENE: Ah, no. I don't believe in telling lies; not in this game. It always comes back on you.

TREB: That's why you're not in parliament, eh?

GENE: I came to this town for one reason: to get your people to vote and in particular for my party. But for the week that I've been here I find no one particularly interested in politics and there isn't an Aboriginal in a decision-making position.

[ELLY *returns and hands* GENE *a cup of tea.*]

Thanks.

ELLY: I am going over to Uncle Blue's: taking him some fish. I'll be back about eight.

TREB: Get some garlic and a couple of spuds. I'll cook the rest of the 'roo later.

GENE: Goodbye, nice meeting you.

[ELLY *leaves.*]

TREB: Aboriginals are not into politics. It's all bullshit.

GENE: It might be bullshit in your opinion, but it's the platform for changing things that you and your supporters desire to alter. You wanna know what's wrong with the old Aboriginal approach to everything?

TREB: I don't wanna know, but I know you're going to tell me anyway.

GENE: I wanna tell you alright. You just don't give a damn about planning things or giving straight answers. You just wait until someone else does something and then you criticise the poor buggers.

TREB: Why should we plan anything? You blokes know better than we do about what's good for us.

GENE: Always an answer, eh? Always an answer. Have you ever asked yourself, 'What can I do for my people?'

TREB: Nothing you can do. Your people are too far gone.

GENE: Real humorous.

TREB: Humour is what helped us survive. We can still laugh after we've seen our land fenced . . . after we've seen our people rot and die in gaols . . . still after we've seen rivers dammed, trees cut down, the ground dug up, the sky filled with dirty smoke . . . still now that you've stripped us of our dignity, shattered our culture, poisoned us with booze . . . You want to take away our humour? Everywhere you go you push your ways of living down the throats of native people.

GENE: Well, what are you going to do about it?

TREB: What can I do?

GENE: Are you asking me or telling yourself? There's about three hundred Aboriginals in this district alone . . . and God knows how many in the electorate. You outnumber us whites three to one at least. So if you wanted to do something, you've got the numbers: all you need is the desire and the ability to communicate with people and a lot of hard work . . . and you can put anyone you want into parliament.

TREB: I am too tired to argue with you right now.

GENE: When then? Just think about what I said: don't leave it for too long.

TREB: Let's meet next Monday after I've finished work . . . about six-ish. Come around for tea.

GENE: Thanks. I look forward to that.

TREB: You're a cheeky bastard.

SCENE TWENTY-ONE

NUMMY *starts on the didgeridoo; the boys go into a dance.*

NUMMY: Let's make this one good. It's our last rehearsal.

TANK: This is going to be bloody good.

NUMMY: While you are sitting still, I've got some news for youse. Know that white fella I was talking to today at Uncle Blue's? Well, he's on the Education Board . . . and he said him and some of the other Board people will be at the ball. And if they like what they see, they will want us to visit all the schools in the area — and maybe schools in Perth, and they will pay us a hundred dollars for every school. We can do two each day.

TANK: Oh boy!

[*He jumps up and dances. He is joined by the others. The lights fade.*]

SCENE TWENTY - TWO

TREB *and* ELLY'*s place, morning.* TREB *tries to wake* NUMMY, *who sleeps on the couch.*

TREB: Nummy, Nummy, get up. I want to talk to you.

NUMMY: Well, today.

TREB: Nummy. I've got to tell you something.

NUMMY: Let me tell you something first. Wait right here.

[NUMMY *exits and returns with a large box.*]

Open it. It's from all of us.

TREB: I'll open it drekley.

NUMMY: No. Open it now, go on.

[TREB *opens the box and produces a guitar.*]

NUMMY: We thought you might want to make a good impression on the school board. It's from all of us.

TREB: Where did youse get the money?

NUMMY: Booked it up. We told old Macy to take it out of our next social cheque. We told him you needed it for tonight.

TREB: You blokes shouldn't have.

NUMMY: I'll see you later. I am going —

TREB: [*interrupting*] Nummy! Just sit down a minute. I've got something to tell you and I don't know how.

NUMMY: Oh, you can tell me anyhow. You know you're my hero.

TREB: Well, shut up and just listen. They don't want you and the boys.

NUMMY: Who don't want us?

TREB: The social committee.

NUMMY: What do you mean, don't want us?

TREB: They don't want youse to perform at the ball.

NUMMY: But everyone just turns up and does anything, and . . .

TREB: Not this year. They're bringing acts from Perth. It's a big event this year — TV and all.

NUMMY: And what's bloody wrong with us? Don't they want any blackfellas? What about you?

TREB: Yeh, well, they want me to sing.

[*Pause.*]

NUMMY: The guitar will look good on TV.

[NUMMY *exits.* TREB *sits still.* ELLY *enters.*]

ELLY: Is Nummy up yet?

TREB: Yes.

ELLY: Did you tell him?

TREB: Yes.

ELLY: How did he take it? Was he alright?

TREB: He seemed okay, but I don't think he was.

ELLY: Whose guitar?

TREB: The boys bought it for me . . . especially for the ball. You know something? I run these blokes down, call them twits, joke about them with my workmates, tease them all the time and I always thought they never liked me. They hang around here because they think Nummy is the

greatest thing since pension days. Then right out of the
blue they go and do something like this.

ELLY: They have always liked you . . . and not only because
you are related to them, either.

TREB: I am going to tell the committee to shove their ball right
up their arse.

ELLY: No you're not. You are representing all of us now, so you
go and show those Perth entertainers what we got.

TREB: You know, I should have went on that committee when
they asked me.

SCENE TWENTY - THREE

GENE *walks past the office. The* NURSE *is sitting quietly.*

GENE: What is happening today?

NURSE: Can't you see? I am in the middle of this big meeting
on the 'Advantages of Cleanliness'. Too many people turned
up, that's why I am having it outside.

[*She starts to weep gently.*]

GENE: Take it easy.

[*He hugs her.*]

NURSE: People just don't care anymore. They are just not
worried how they live. For the whole three months in this
town, I have worked bloody hard . . . yet I am still a
stranger.

GENE: I think a lot of us have been working hard in the wrong
direction. Sorry, I don't mean our intentions are not right
or just. Have you been to any of the local functions?

NURSE: No.

GENE: Nor have I. From one stranger to another, would you
accompany me to the ball?

NURSE: Yes, why not?

[*To her invisible audience.*]

Well, the meeting is broken up and youse can all go and get
fucked.

SCENE TWENTY - FOUR

TREB *and* ELLY'*s place, late afternoon.* TARA *adjusts herself.*

TARA: I'm here to pick you up. How long you gunna be there?

ELLY: [*off*] Treb is in the shower. I'll be out in a tick.

TARA: Hey, whose guitar?

ELLY: [*off*] Treb's. The boys bought it for him. It's deadly, eh?

TARA: Yeh. I seen all the boys heading to the hall. All dolled up — you wouldn't know them. All sober too. I forgot how handsome those blokes was.

[ELLY *enters.*]

ELLY: Was Nummy with them?

TARA: Come to think of it, no.

ELLY: Did they all get the news?

TARA: Yeh. They said they didn't care — they didn't want to dance anyway, they reckon. But you could see the disappointment on their faces.

ELLY: I'm worried about Nummy.

TARA: Don't worry about Nummy, he can look after himself. He's a tough nut.

ELLY: He's a nut alright — very brittle inside.

TREB: [*off*] Where's my shoes, Elly?

ELLY: On the small cupboard near the bed.

TARA: Hurry up! The thing will be starting soon.

TREB: [*off*] I'm coming.

SCENE TWENTY - FIVE

The lights go up on a stump. NUMMY, *drunk, talks and sings to himself.*

NUMMY: A man is better off by himself. Who wanted to go to the dance anyway? Blackfellas, eh? dressing up . . .

[GINNA *approaches.*]

GINNA: Hey, *coordah*!

NUMMY: Who's that?

GINNA: Me, *coordah*.

NUMMY: Hey, Ginna. How you going, my *coordah*?

GINNA: I was worried about you.

NUMMY: Don't have to worry about me: you should be at the ball — You look *moordich*, boy!

GINNA: No, I wanna be with you. Tell me some more of those yarns. I like them.

NUMMY: No, you go and enjoy yourself.

GINNA: But this is my good fun. I wish I was with you all those times, when you did all them things.

NUMMY: Come on. Looks like I am gunna have to go with you. Come on, let's go to the ball and I'll spit on the dinner table.

SCENE TWENTY - SIX

KOOLBARDI *dances on, then sits on a log.* JUNE *approaches and sits near him.*

JUNE: Knew I'd catch you here. Can you read them? The stars?

KOOLBARDI: Sure can.

JUNE: Can you teach me?

KOOLBARDI: What would you like me to teach you?

JUNE: To read the stars.

KOOLBARDI: Oh, I thought you wanted to learn something else.

JUNE: Such as?

KOOLBARDI: Wouldn't have a clue.

JUNE: You don't really trust me, do you?

KOOLBARDI: Do you trust me?

JUNE: Sure, why not? You know what is the biggest problem in the world?

KOOLBARDI: No. But you gunna tell me.

JUNE: Communication which is achieved through trust. Communication between nations, between race . . .

[*Pause.*]

And communication between two people.

[JUNE *sits closer.*]

If people are honest with each other and talk about their life styles, and their outlooks on life, it develops an understanding between them. Ignorance creates prejudice. You and I can really get to understand each other. We can really help our people to get along together . . . live in harmony. But we must be honest to ourselves. True to each other. No secrets.

KOOLBARDI: Do you know what you're saying?

JUNE: Yes.

KOOLBARDI: Do you realise how dangerous this could be?

JUNE: It's going to happen anyway. Nothing stands still. What is life without risks, challenges?

KOOLBARDI: Why don't people just leave things as they are? Why do they cut up animals to see what's inside them? What for? Then they experiment on us.

JUNE: What do you mean?

KOOLBARDI: Nothing.

[*Pause.*]

JUNE: Look at me. We *can* help each other. They are giving the women pills, aren't they? And what are they doing to the kids? I'll find out, then I'll expose the whole ugly story.

KOOLBARDI: You know about the pills? What do they do?

JUNE: I don't know yet. But I'll find out. Peter, there's a lot of bitterness, confusion and mistrust boiling inside you. Let it out.

KOOLBARDI: If we take the best from my people and the best from your people, we could make something good here.

JUNE: We sure can.

KOOLBARDI: And if we expose all the bad points . . . that should stop them, 'cause everyone will know what they are doing.

JUNE: That they will.

KOOLBARDI: I will show you some things.

JUNE: And I will show you some things.

END OF ACT ONE

ACT TWO

SCENE ONE

The NURSE and GENE enter.

NURSE: I haven't had a barn dance for years.

GENE: Yeh, it showed.

NURSE: Ooooh.

GENE: But you waltzed divinely . . . It was a good night, wasn't it?

NURSE: Sure was. Wonder what caused the malfunction. Did you see Treb protecting his new guitar?

GENE: He's not a bad bloke, Treb. Nice family, too. God, they have it tough. When I was sent up here I expected to see something different. You know why I came up here? I'm the advance bunnie . . . sent to lure the darkies' vote. Wait a minute!

NURSE: What's wrong?

GENE: Nothing wrong at all. Not a thing wrong. [*To an imaginary figure*] Excuse me, Mister Mighty Party Leader. Mister Bartholom M.L.A.O. of A., J.P. and Ph.D.

NURSE: M.T.T.

GENE: T.A.A., U.D.L., O.T.C., R.A.C.

NURSE: U.S.S.R.

GENE: C.S.I.R.O., K.G.B. and C.I.A. Sir. [*Pointing*] Report from the North.

    [NURSE *redirects his arm.*]

The North. All the Aborigines are going to vote, the whole mob of 'em, by the truckload [*to* NURSE] But not for who he thinks they're going to vote for . . . Treb, M.P. Yes, mate, you and I can pull it off.

NURSE: Gene . . . would you like a coffee?

GENE: Yeah, why not?

    [*They exit.*]

SCENE TWO

The lights go up on TREB *and* ELLY's *place. From off comes lots of noise.* ELLY *enters, followed by* TREB, *then* GINNA.

TREB: What a night!
  [ELLY *laughs.*]
ELLY: I loved it when those fire sprinklers started. Everyone in
  the hall got soaked.
TREB: Yes . . . I wonder what happened. Must have been a
  malfunction.
GINNA: Wasn't that hard.
ELLY: What you mean, wasn't hard?
TREB: Come on . . . what do you know about it?
GINNA: I don't know anything. I promised Nummy I wouldn't
  tell.
TREB: Nummy — of course!
ELLY: How did Nummy do it? Come on, you can tell us. It was
  a good trick. One of his best.
TREB: Yeh . . . that Nummy is deadly, *unna*?
GINNA: Yeh . . . he's *moordich*. Only him could'a thought of
  putting a heater next to it.
ELLY: But I didn't see Nummy there.
GINNA: He came through the back door when I opened it . . .
  and then he went again. So I helped him, too.
TREB: And then last week Tank and Nummy had a fight at
  Uncle Blue's.
ELLY: Yeh . . . I heard. Tank flogged him.
TREB: Yeh. Nummy would shape up karate style and Tank
  would just lift him.
GINNA: But Nummy didn't want to hurt him. He could have
  killed him with a karate kick.
TREB: Yeh . . . But Nummy waited till Tank flaked out and
  you know what he done?
ELLY: No, what?
TREB: He pulled Tank's trousers off and then he went to the
  stove and got the pot off which had curry beef in it and

tipped it into Tank's jocks. Then pulled his trousers back on. When Tank woke up he thought he shit himself. Gees it was funny! You should have been there to see how Tank tried to walk! 'What's up, Tank?' Nummy said, 'Oh, nothing,' he said.

ELLY: Oh well! Let's hit the sack. I am bushed.

GINNA: I'll wait for Nummy.

ELLY: No you won't. You go to bed now!

[*The lights fade.*]

SCENE THREE

The lights go up on TREB *and* ELLY's *place, morning.* GINNA *sits on the lounge.* TREB *walks in and puts the kettle on.*

GINNA: Morning . . .

TREB: What you doing up this early?

GINNA: I stayed up. My *coordah* Nummy never come home.

TREB: Don't you worry about him. He'll be alright.

GINNA: He worries about me.

[ELLY *enters.*]

ELLY: Who you talking to?

[TREB *nods toward* GINNA.]

What you doing up?

GINNA: Waiting for my *coordah.*

ELLY: Oh. He's okay. I am sure. Kettle on?

TREB: Yeh . . . I'll come home for dinner.

[*The phone rings.* TREB *answers.*]

Hello. yeh, she's up. [*To* ELLY] It's for you.

ELLY: Hello . . . yes . . . What? When? Is he alright? What happened?

TREB: What's up?

ELLY: Nummy's in hospital. He's been hit by a car. He's in a coma.

[ELLY *bursts into tears. There is a knock on the door.* TREB *opens it.* TARA *walks in, goes to* ELLY *and comforts her.*]

I just found out. I took Aunty Flo up to see the doctor and they told me.

TREB: Did they say what happened?

TARA: It was a hit and run. He was hit some time late last night and they never took him to hospital till this morning.

TREB: You mean he laid there all fucken night and no one seen him?

TARA: Apparently Jack Winter and a couple of other people saw him, but thought he was drunk and flaked out. They reckon they have seen him like that before. Then when Jack was going to clean the hall this morning he saw him again — so he went over to wake him up and noticed blood on his face. Then he called the ambulance. Jack was still at the hospital when I arrived.

TREB: Every time they see a blackfellow laying down they reckon he's drunk. Never sick or injured. Always fucken drunk.

ELLY: I'll have a wash, then go and see him.

[ELLY *walks out.* TREB *goes to the phone and rings.*]

TREB: Hello June . . . this is Treb. Will you tell Graham that I won't be at work today? Tell him there has been an accident involving the family. No . . . Elly's okay. It's her brother, Nummy. He was hit by a car and is in hospital . . . Thanks June. [*To* TARA] Do they know who hit him?

GINNA: Old Morgan, I bet! I'll kill that old bastard!

TARA: No, they don't know and it may not have been Morgan, so don't you go jumping to conclusions.

GINNA: It would be him alright! He's the only one who drives around here drunk.

TARA: Nearly the whole town was drunk last night!

[ELLY *reappears.* TREB *cuddles her and together they walk out.*]

GINNA: Is he gunna die?

TARA: No! He's as tough as nails.

SCENE FOUR

BROTHER DAVIS *talks to* JILLAWARRA *and KOOLBARDI.*

DAVIS: It's not as simple as that. You have to look really deep to find the answer. The only place to find it is in the Bible. The Bible —

JILLAWARRA: [*interrupting*] Just a minute, brother. You always tell us to look to the Bible: it has everything in there. Then how come it say one thing then say another that mean different.

DAVIS: The Bible does not contradict itself.

JILLAWARRA: Then how come it say 'turn the other cheek', then also 'an eye for an eye'? It say 'love your enemy', yet how many enemy was killed in wars?

DAVIS: But you must look at the context of when these things take place. At times there is justification for killing.

JILLAWARRA: You tell us it's wrong when we carry out our law.

DAVIS: That is different.

JILLAWARRA: How?

DAVIS: That takes a lot of explanation, but right now let's settle this problem.

KOOLBARDI: It's not a problem. We'll just spear him.

DAVIS: I'll have none of that talk.

JILLAWARRA: But that's our way.

DAVIS: There will be no spears thrown on my mission.

JILLAWARRA: I thought it was our mission, Mister Davis.

DAVIS: Yours, ours, mine . . . it makes no difference. There will be no spearing.

KOOLBARDI: We'll just throw boomerangs at him, then.

DAVIS: No spears, no boomerangs.

KOOLBARDI: Rocks?

JILLAWARRA: Shut up. This is serious. If you can't be serious, then shut up.
    [*Pause.*]
He's not getting away with it.

DAVIS: You'll find a punishment to suit the crime.

KOOLBARDI: Who's going to tell us that?

DAVIS: The Lord's going to tell us that.

KOOLBARDI: And how he gunna tell us? Newspaper or pedal radio?

JILLAWARRA: [*to* KOOLBARDI] *Dubbarkunl darwoora dubbaakung lngunl barking barming* . . . you bloody idiot! (*To* DAVIS] Mister Davis, I never ask this before. Out of respect for you I never asked — I know about you more than you think I know. Why is your way always right? Your God and our God have the same law. We say we one with the earth — she my mother. You don't believe that. But you say 'ashes to ashes, dust to dust'; same thing. When you see my people worship the spirits at our sacred places you say it no good. No good to worship the trees and the rocks. Yet you cut the trees down and make a building, shape the rocks to make altar, then you worship your spirits.

DAVIS: Men are made different. Some men could never see . . . come to terms with their conscience — they believe they and their spirit are separate, not one.

KOOLBARDI: *Schizophrenics.*

DAVIS: They tell me we poisoned your brain. I think we may have removed it.

JILLAWARRA: Right.

> [*Pause.*]

You don't realise how true it is.

SCENE FIVE

The hospital. NUMMY *sits up in bed.* GINNA *walks in.*

GINNA: Hey, *coordah*!

NUMMY: Ginna!

GINNA: Did Elly and Treb come in today?

NUMMY: Yeh. You know Elly. She's been in every day. I told her not to worry. I'll be out tomorrow.

GINNA: But you only woke up yesterday.

NUMMY: Yeh, well, I needed a rest, see. So I thought if I slept for a week that would be enough rest all at once instead of every now and then.

GINNA: I knew you was smarter than these doctors.

NUMMY: Did you bring my medicine?

GINNA: Your port?

NUMMY: Slip it under the pillow.

GINNA: Why you didn't know me yesterday?

NUMMY: Well, you know when you wake up from sleep, you feel tired and you have to start thinking again? Sometimes you forget what day it is . . .

GINNA: Yeh . . .

NUMMY: Well, I had a long sleep and I forgot a lot of things. When I woke up yesterday, I didn't know who I was. Then it all came back to me.

    [*Pause.*]

Slowly.

GINNA: Old Morgan went to court this morning.

NUMMY: Old bastard!

GINNA: How did you remember wine?

NUMMY: [*smiling*] Some things you never forget.

GINNA: Then you remembered me, too?

NUMMY: Sort of . . . Yeh.

GINNA: Did you remember Uncle Blue?

NUMMY: Uncle who?

GINNA: Uncle Blue . . . You still don't remember him?

NUMMY: Yeh, I know him. I am only teasing you.

    [TREB *enters.*]

TREB: Hey, *coordah*! What you up to?

NUMMY: Yeh, where you come from?

TREB: I just came from the court house. You know what you're worth? Three months' suspension and one hundred dollars fine!

NUMMY: Well, that's only three months less than poor old cuz.

GINNA: Cuz who?

TREB: Uncle Dave's eldest son.

GINNA: What happened?

TREB: Cuz, rest in peace, had a fight with Mick Lewis.

GINNA: The farmer?

TREB: Yes . . . Anyway, cuz flogged Mick, left him laying in the bar. Then while he was walking home later, Mick drove his car onto the curb and run cuz down — killing him!

GINNA: And did they hang him?

TREB: No. Six months' suspension and one hundred dollars fine.

NUMMY: But I made Mick piss in jail. I would have killed him if the police didn't stop me. Then they made me piss.

GINNA: Dirty bastards! Wish I was there.

[*The lights fade.*]

SCENE SIX

The lights go up on the kitchen at ELLY *and* TREB's *place.* ELLY *and* TREB *sit at the table.* TARA *walks in.*

ELLY: Morning.

TARA: Morning. He's run away!

TREB: Who?

TARA: Nummy. He's run away from hospital. Last night.

TREB: What nurse did he run away with?

ELLY: It's not funny. He's a very sick man!

TARA: And, they found two empty wine bottles in his bin.

ELLY: How did he get them?

TREB: You don't want me to tell you . . . eh . . . really!

[ELLY *heads off to* GINNA's *room.*]

ELLY: Ginna. I am gunna wake him up and jar him.

[*She exits.*]

TREB: Well, I am off to work. See youse tonight.

[ELLY *comes in again.*]

ELLY: Ginna never slept in his bed.

TREB: He's probably with Nummy.

ELLY: Then you better go and look for them.

TREB: Hey! I got work to do. Don't worry, they'll come home when they're hungry.

TARA: I'll have a look for them.

TREB: Elly, love, they'll be okay.

ELLY: I hope so!

TREB: If they're not back by the time I knock off, I'll know where to find them.

ELLY: Yeh, I suppose they're alright. The more you worry about them two, the worse they get.

SCENE SEVEN

A bush clearing with a log. KOOLBARDI *enters followed by* JILLAWARRA. KOOLBARDI *stops, centre. They stare at each other. Pause.*

KOOLBARDI: What I did was wrong — but we were only trying to —

JILLAWARRA: [*interrupting*] It doesn't matter now.

KOOLBARDI: Of course it matters. They're gunna find out now. We can still hide the secrets of the rain, the secret of the river and the secrets of the marriage . . . all the secrets, we can hide them all. I want to make a better life for us all.

[*Pause.*]

I didn't know she was gunna show the world. I did not want to hurt my people . . . I just want us and them to understand each other. Communicate. No secrets, no ignorance.

[*Pause.*]

I want to make a better life for us all.

JILLAWARRA: Did you really think that white woman would stay with you? Did you really think she would take you back to the city? Has she ever been seen with you? Has she even seen you in the day? . . . Think about it . . . Did she really care for you, or a good story?

KOOLBARDI: I am ready. [*He rises and walks to the log. He returns to* JILLAWARA.) Take care of Mum.

The bush. JUNE *enters.*

JUNE: Peter? . . . Peter ! . . . Peter! . . .
 [JILLAWARRA *enters.*]
 Where's Peter? Have you seen the —
JILLAWARRA: [*interrupting*] I know.
JUNE: How could you know? I just got these magazines off the plane. They're not even released yet.
JILLAWARRA: You don't even know what you've done, do you?
JUNE: Of course I do. I have exposed the native welfare department.
JILLAWARRA: And the pictures, and about our law . . . Why you did this?
JUNE: That's how you get things published. You feed them the mysterious tales, then they print the real issue.
JILLAWARRA: Just mysterious tales?
JUNE: Where's Peter?
JILLAWARRA: Koolbardi. His name is 'Koolbardi'. There's nothing you can do for him now.
JUNE: What have youse done to him?
JILLAWARRA: We do nothing. He knows.
JUNE: What have youse done to him?
JILLAWARRA: You will never understand how much damage you have done. You have destroyed more than a life.
JUNE: Listen . . . you paganistic . . .
JILLAWARRA: Don't push your luck.
JUNE: You're just jealous. Youse have always hated him because he's smarter than youse, different than youse. That's why you hate him.
JILLAWARRA: Hate him! I could never hate him. He's my brother — my *coordah*.

SCENE NINE

The front of TREB *and* ELLY'*s house.* ELLY *and* TARA *enter.*

ELLY: People around here would never believe how smart Nummy was. He used to be the fastest runner in the whole area.

TARA: What happened?

ELLY: Had a tough life. When he got out of the army he just drank himself silly.

TARA: I didn't know Nummy was in the army.

ELLY: His best friend was killed, right before his eyes.
    [TREB *enters.*]

TREB: Find them?

TARA: Not yet.

TREB: I know where they are.

SCENE TEN

NUMMY *shadow boxes at the log. The* NURSE *enters, but doesn't see him.* NUMMY *spots her coming and sits down and mumbles as if in a trance. The* NURSE *approaches and walks around him.* NUMMY *wakes up.*

NUMMY: Hey . . . how long you been here?

NURSE: About two minutes. What are you doing?

NUMMY: Travelling.

NURSE: Travelling?

NUMMY: Yeh, travelling.

NURSE: Where to?

NUMMY: Anywhere and everywhere. Once you close your mind and let your spirit take over, you can do anything you like. Go anywhere.

NURSE: Like astral travel? Exploration of the universe?

NUMMY: Yeh — sort of. But more stronger than that . . . its —

NURSE: [*interrupting*] Or like autosuggestion. You can heal yourself and strengthen your body by applying your mind.

You explore your inner self. You attack any virus or injury with waves of positive thoughts — er — vibes. You alienate any negative thoughts.

NUMMY: Yeh . . . sorta like that!

NURSE: That's how you also attract other people to you, isn't it? You connect your thought waves with theirs. You bombard their thoughts with images of yourself, until you are all they can think about.

NUMMY: Yeh, that's what I was doing. I was seeing if it worked on white women.

NURSE: Anyone I know?

NUMMY: You know her very well. She's very close to you.

NURSE: Give me a hint. Ah, you can't, it'll break the connection.

NUMMY: No it won't. It's you. I have been thinking about you all day. Positive thoughts. That's what drew you here.

NURSE: No. I came to see if anyone was going to come to a meeting.

NUMMY: You knew I was here, didn't you? And all by myself. You are a really lovely woman. Nice legs. Nice bum. Come here and give me a kiss. You must be mad about me by now.

NURSE: I have to go!

[*She retreats from him.*]

NUMMY: Don't fight it, baby. It's stronger than me and you. It's our good vibes. We belong together like a signature and a social cheque. We could sail away together on that sea of wine in a boat made of love.

[*She exits.*]

We can —

[*He falls off the log.*]

Shit! What am I saying? I can't swim . . . But I'd have a bloody good time drowning.

[GINNA *enters and approaches the prone* NUMMY.]

GINNA: *Coordah.* You wanna know what?

NUMMY: Hmmm . . .

GINNA: I wish I was a young bloke with you.

NUMMY: You are!

GINNA: What?

NUMMY: You're a young bloke and you're with me now!

GINNA: No, I mean I wish —

NUMMY: [*interrupting*] Yes, I know: you wanted to be a teenager with me . . .

GINNA: Yeh.

NUMMY: Well, you are a teen.

GINNA: No!

NUMMY: Yeh, I know. I am only teasing.

GINNA: Yeh. I want to be like you. Will you teach me all the jokes you know? And all those Nyoongah songs and dances, and all those stories. Tell them to me again! About the time you was in the war and how you played football.

NUMMY: It's all bullshit. Only songs I know are dirty ones. When shots was fired at me I shit myself — and I was always on the reverse in football sides . . . and I never ever won a raffle.

GINNA: See? . . . you always say something funny.

NUMMY: *Coordah.* Ever tried to catch your thumb like this?

[NUMMY *shows* GINNNA *how to try to catch his thumb which is impossible.*]

But you only got five shots.

GINNA: Okay, I'll do it in four.

[NUMMY *lies down:* GINNA *tries hard but with no success.*]

Give me three more goes.

[*He tries again.*]

Huh, it's impossible. You know, it's right here in front of my eyes but I just can't grab it. You know, *coordah* . . . there's a lot of things like that — you can see but can't grab.

[*Pause.*]

Coordah?

[GINNA *turns around and sees* NUMMY *lying still.*]

Coordah, lots of people think I am silly. Reckon I should stay in the home doing those paintings — putting red tops here and the blue ones there — but you showed them. You showed them, *coordah, coordah.* They say I got no feeling, but you showed them, *coordah.*

THE END

GLOSSARY

The Aboriginal language used in *Coordah* is usually called Nyoongah but occasionally referred to as Bibbulman. Nyoongah literally means 'man', but has become a general term denoting Aboriginality in the South West of Western Australia. Bibbulman is one of the fourteen South West languages that have combined over the last 152 years to create the modern Nyoongah spoken in the play.

COORDAH, brother
CARDA, racehorse goanna
KARTWORRA, mad, bad head
KOOLBARDI, magpie
MOONARCH, police
MOORDICH, good
NYUMBI, type of dance
WUDJELLAS, whitemen

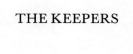

THE KEEPERS

Above: Annie Hanlon as Elizabeth Campbell, Lillian Crombie as Mirnat, Christopher Williams as Michael Campbell. Below: Lillian Crombie and Lew Cleaver as Daniel. Aboriginal National Theatre Trust production. Photos: Brenda Croft.

The Keepers was first performed by the Mainstreet Theatre Company in the Town Hall, Naracoorte, South Australia on 25 February, 1988 with the following cast:

KOONAWAR/DANIEL	Michael Johnson
MIRNAT/LILLIPA	Betty Sumner
REVEREND JAMES ROEBURNE/MICHAEL/ VESSY/McGUINESS/ MAYOR	Ian Pidd
ELIZABETH ROEBURNE/ MISS MURCHISON	Fiona Barber

Directed by Geoff Crowhurst

The play was subsequently revised and performed at Troupe Theatre in Adelaide as part of the 1988 Adelaide Festival, and a later production by the Aboriginal National Theatre Trust was presented at Belvoir Street Theatre in Sydney. The script presented here has been further revised by the author.

CHARACTERS

KOONAWAR, a tribal elder of the Boandik tribe

MIRNAT, wife of Koonawar

DANIEL, son of Koonawar and Mirmat, in his twenties

REVEREND JAMES CAMPBELL, a Scottish missionary, in his thirties

ELIZABETH CAMPBELL, James Campbell's wife, in her late twenties

MICHAEL CAMPBELL, son of James and Elizabeth, in his twenties

McGUINNESS, a policeman in his thirties or early forties

VESSY, a bullock driver

LILLIPA JEFFREY, a young Aboriginal girl

McELVOY, Daniel's boss

There is also a white baby and an Aboriginal baby in Act One, the children of James and Elizabeth, and Koonawar and Mirmat. In Act Two Mirmat and Elizabeth are aged in their fifties. In the last scene, Mirmat and Elizabeth are old ladies in their seventies.

SETTING

The Keepers is set in the middle of the nineteenth century on the south-east coast of South Australia. The indigenous people are the Boandik, a proud and gentle people. It is the period of European settlement, and the inevitable confrontation of cultures has a devastating effect upon the Boandik.

ACT ONE

SCENE ONE

Two figures in leotards emerge from opposite sides of the stage. One is dressed completely in black, the other white. As the stage lightens, an Aboriginal chant is heard in the distance, accompanied by rhythm sticks. The white dancer freezes. The black dancer performs a dance of the home of the Boandik, then freezes. The Aboriginal chant fades out and slow, distant Scottish bagpipes are heard. The white dancer performs a dance of Scotland. Distant thunder sounds. The dancer freezes. An Aborigine laughs and calls out in Boandik. The black dancer performs a courting dance of the Boandik, then freezes. A Scot laughs and calls out in Gaelic. The white dancer performs a Scottish courting dance, then freezes. The thunder sounds closer, interspersed with bagpipes. There is a loud heartbeat, and the white dancer performs a symbolic dance of white childbirth in a hospital bed, reaching a climax with the cry of the newborn. The white dancer exits. The black dancer performs a symbolic dance of Boandik childbirth, which is sitting up. This climaxes with the cry of the newborn and the dancer exits. Moonlight touches the leaves of the bulrushes. The night is alive with the life of the swamp. Off, a curlew calls and a woman's laugh breaks the silence. She is a new mother, proud of her achievement. The baby cries softly. Pause. MIRNAT *enters carrying a baby wrapped in skins. She is still in black leotards, but now wears a kangaroo or wallaby skin. She comes to the fireplace and puts the baby down, then goes to the sea to wash herself. She is physically drained. She returns and drinks thirstily from a coolamon and eats hungrily the berries and other food from her dillybag. From this little distance she studies her newborn child inquisitively and speaks to him in Boandik. She takes a final bite and drink and goes again to the baby. She holds him to the firelight to study him more closely. Lights crossfade to another area where* ELIZABETH, *the Scottish mother, still in white leotards, also studies her child. She is draped in a shawl or some other simple costume which implies the character. The Aboriginal mother sings 'Warinor'; the Scottish mother sings 'Brae Toraetor.' Though ages and distances apart, the songs harmonise. Slow fade to blackout.*

SCENE TWO

The Koonowar camp, day. MIRNAT *sits grinding seed for bread. As she works she seems contented. She places the damper in the ashes and moves about doing other chores such as basket or string making. Slowly she becomes aware of a sound that only she hears. It is eerie. She turns her head to listen, then returns to her chore. A second, barely audible cry catches her attention. She sits with her head down, listening hard. Nothing. Another unheard sound propels her to her feet. Bristling, she turns to seek out the unseen intruder.* KOONOWAR, *a strong young warrior, enters behind her. She pays no attention. He is dressed in a black leotard with a string belt and the suggestion of a possum skin loincloth, and carries a fighting stick. He walks in front of her, but she continues to look past him. He turns to see what she is looking at.*

KOONOWAR: [*gently*] What did you see?
MIRNAT: I thought I heard someone call my name . . .
    [*She returns to her work.*]
  I was probably hearing something else.
    [KOONOWAR *sits opposite her and takes up a half-finished spear. She looks at him.*]
  I felt sort of cold all of a sudden . . . I'm being silly, eh?
KOONOWAR: No. I don't think you're silly at all.
    [*He rises and, almost nonchalantly, moves up behind her. He pounces.*]
  She *moogada.*
    [*The birth of the baby is the end of a nine month drought for* KOONOWAR. *His ardour is keen.*]
MIRNAT: Ay, get out, you . . . Go on, leave me now . . . Stop that, Koonowar . . . Hey, I'll burn you with a fire . . . That'll cool ya down.
    [*He moves out of range. They both sit poised, playing the age old game of boy and girl.*]
  Go on, plenty time for that later . . . Go and do some work. Go get me some fish. Go on now, ya *boodoo.*

[*He feints at her a couple of times, then good-naturedly returns to his spear making. He becomes absorbed in thought.*]

KOONOWAR: I was over at the Karaal water today, see if I could get some *keil*.

MIRNAT: Ay, wrong time. They nesting now . . . Anyway, did you get anything?

KOONOWAR: Nothing . . . While I was there, I met old Karim, the lizard man.

MIRNAT: What, that madman from the Mootatunga people? He's crazy . . . *wirangy*. What're you talking to him for?

KOONOWAR: He's not that silly.

MIRNAT: No . . . he wouldn't sound mad to you, eh? You're both a bit *wirangy*.

[*Drums sound in the distance.* KOONOWAR *goes quiet.*]

Ay, Koonowar . . . Ay, I was only joking, come on . . .

KOONOWAR: I'm not worried about that. It's what Karim was telling me.

[MIRNAT *notes his seriousness and goes back to her work. She waits in the knowledge that what* KOONOWAR *has to say he will say in good time.* KOONOWAR *walks up and back, then stands near* MIRNAT *and looks into the distance. His voice becomes that of the storyteller.*]

The branches of the *munter* will have good apples . . . at first . . . but then . . . they will all begin to fall off . . . before they are ripe . . . and will rot on the ground . . . Even their seeds will rot. The green apples on the tree will begin to get a disease on them. They'll be covered in . . . this . . . *white dust*. More white than our whitest clay. That dust is sickness . . . and that sickness will choke the fruit . . . so that it will either fall to the ground and rot away like the other ones . . . or it will stay on the tree . . . all twisted and ugly . . . with that rotting disease all over it. That's what Karim said to me.

MIRNAT: I told you. You shouldn't listen to that old man . . . He's *boontha*.

KOONOWAR: A big wind is coming, he said . . . Really big . . . Bringing this white dust with it and that white dust is going to cover all the fruit trees . . . the ground, rocks, everything

. . . He said a lot of things going to die from that dust . . .
Even man.

MIRNAT: Stop it, Koonowar . . . You starting to frighten me.

[KOONOWAR *comforts her.*]

KOONOWAR: Karim isn't talking about a real dust storm.
That's just his version . . . the picture he must get in his
head. It's like a warning of what could happen.

[MIRNAT *settles down and* KOONOWAR *returns to his spear.*]

That white dust storm could be anything . . . the wind . . .
could be lightning. He told me another thing about a journey some of his people made. Some time ago, three
Mootatunga men followed the sun-up for a good many
days. They came to this camp. In that camp were two
walim.

MIRNAT: [*apprehensively*] Spirit people?

KOONOWAR: Same one. When those men saw the *walim* they
ran away and hid, but the spirits didn't chase them, so the
three sneaked back . . .

MIRNAT: I tell you . . . men can be real fools when they want
to be . . . Sorry, go on.

KOONOWAR: So they sneaked back and they watched the two
spirit . . . For a long time they lay down there watching
them two . . . Now this is the strange part. Karim always
said that the *walim* must be spirits of the *karato* . . .

MIRNAT: The snake?

KOONOWAR: They can change their skin like a snake. Just . . .
like . . . a . . . snake.

[MIRNAT *is agitated.*]

MIRNAT: Koonowar, what's all this talk?

[KOONOWAR *becomes pensive. He rises to his feet and begins
moving about.*]

KOONOWAR: I think what the old man told me is true. You
remember that man, he came back from the big water that
time . . . What's his name?

MIRNAT: Bora? . . . But they thought he was *wirangy* too, from
eating too much poison shell.

KOONOWAR: I don't think he was. You remember he said he's
seen the *walim* smash their canoe on the rocks and they

jumped in the water and came out on to the sand . . . and
then . . . just like a snake . . . they pulled their skin off . . .
and Bora said they were white . . . like a snake with a new
skin.

MIRNAT: Koonowar, don't talk about it . . . you making my
hair stand.

KOONOWAR: I'm not trying to frighten you . . . but we have to
listen to the warnings . . . We have to get ourselves ready. If
those . . . *snake people* want to try and come to our country
. . . we'll have to fight.

[*Fade to blackout.*]

SCENE THREE

The beach, day. There is a large box. Oars with rowlocks attached rest
nearby with other items that suggest arrival at an early settlement. The
sea is heard on the beach, with gulls perhaps and a sea breeze in the trees.
ELIZABETH *enters, trying to cool herself and her child from the warm*
sun. Still in leotards, she wears a skirt, a neck bodice, sleeve pieces
suitable for quick changes, perhaps a broad straw hat held with a scarf,
and white slip-ons. She finds a shady place for the infant, sits, cools
herself and waves away the flies. JAMES *enters. He wears a loose, long-*
sleeved shirt, a black ribbon tie and a black mormon-type hat and black
shoes. He carries bags which he deposits near the box and surveys the
terrain.

JAMES: Can you believe it, Elizabeth? Our own world at last.
Virtually untouched by civilization . . . Look there, quick.
What creature is that?

[ELIZABETH *joins him.*]

ELIZABETH: It's a kangaroo . . . Oh, there's another over there
near those bushes.

JAMES: Lord be praised . . . Elizabeth, just look at all those
birds and those fish in the sea . . . Will you look at those
birds . . . I've never seen the likes . . . Oh, my dear
Elizabeth . . . what a grand place . . .

[*He strides around enthusiastically.*]

Yes . . . a fine home for our children . . . We'll build our
house on that ridge there . . . and there's good lumber here
for building . . . and on that slope in that little cove there,
we'll build our kirk. Oh, Elizabeth, this has been my dream
for so long . . . How I've waited for this . . .

ELIZABETH: [*quietly*] James . . .

JAMES: Aye, my love?

ELIZABETH: Have we . . . ?

JAMES: Yes, Elizabeth? . . . 'Have we . . ' what?

ELIZABETH: Have we made the right decision?

[JAMES' *enthusiasm wanes. He comes to her thoughtfully and,
giving her a gentle look, moves around pensively.*]

JAMES: [*with conviction*] In our time together I've never
promised you anything I've not been able to give. I've not
guaranteed anything . . . and I've no guarantee now. All I
can promise you is that anything we do . . . we do together.
I have a belief. I believe we are doing the right thing. I
believe we are being guided by the hand of the Almighty
and we will be protected. That belief gives me the strength
to do many things . . . and with your strength as well . . .
we have a great future here.

ELIZABETH: Forgive me, James. Sometimes I feel . . . a little
unsure of myself. Then I look at you and I feel good again.
You are my strength.

[*She moves to gaze over the sea.*]

I've never regretted being with you. I've never doubted you
for a moment. Making the decision to leave Scotland . . .
was very hard for me . . . against the wishes of my parents,
my friends. They believed I'd taken leave of my senses,
going off to strange corners of the earth . . . with a *wee
bairn*.

JAMES: Elizabeth, I didn't wish for —

ELIZABETH: [*interrupting*] Let me finish, James . . . please.

[*She gathers her thoughts.* JAMES *stands apart.*]

I thought about it. I had the choice. One day at one of
Mother's garden parties I met Mrs Courtiers, who gave me
a book about the journals of Captain James Cook . . .

JAMES: I didn't know you were interested in adventure stories.

ELIZABETH: I'm not, particularly . . . but what moved me was the Captain's deep regret that he'd never given his family . . . a family life. To his children . . . he had grown a stranger. To his wife . . . an intruder. So I decided then and there, James Campbell . . . wither thou goest . . . go I . . . and our son.

> [JAMES *is moved. He looks long and deep at her, struggling to contain his feelings. He turns to the goods.*]

JAMES: We're nae going to have a store and parish this way. I'd best start putting up the tent.

ELIZABETH: I'll settle Michael under the shade and give you a hand.

> [*They move to set up camp when a voice calls from behind them. They turn, but no one is to be seen.* JAMES *walks out and surveys the terrain in the heavy silence. Fade to blackout.*]

SCENE FOUR

The Koonowar camp, day. All is quiet. MIRNAT *enters carrying a dillybag of wild foods tied to her head and resting in the crook of her back. In one arm she carries a coolamon which holds her baby, wrapped in skins. In the other she carries her digging stick and some firewood tied with sinew. She throws down the wood and, holding the handle of the coolamon, swings it off her back and puts it on the ground without disturbing her sleeping child. She puts the babe in the cool of the gunyah and stands and stretches. She takes in the fresh air and basks in the warm setting sun. She hears the eerie sound again and is immediately on guard. She quickly moves to protect her child. She hears the noise first to her left, then her right and suddenly all around her in the ground and in the air. She flattens herself against the ground to listen. From the distance comes the sound of large animals approaching through the bush. Suddenly the sound of a herd of cattle and its drovers fill her world. She is cornered like an animal, unable to go forward or back. Petrified, she clings to the safety of her house. Gradually the sounds diminish, till all is again quiet.*

SCENE FIVE

The Koonowar camp, twilight. The sounds of the bush at the end of the day are heard. Timidly, MIRNAT *comes out of her gunyah and gets something to eat. She is like a cat on wet grass, trying to get things done without too much noise.* KOONOWAR *bursts into the camp with a leg of mutton, freshly killed. She nearly dies. He has seen the cattle also. He drops the barely noticed mutton and quickly goes to her. She nestles safely to him without a word. They sit on the ground in front of the gunyah, the only sound* MIRNAT's *soft sobbing. He sits stiffly, staring into the distance. Fade to blackout.*

SCENE SIX

The Campbell camp, dusk. The lean-to now serves as a store. JAMES *takes stock by the oil lamps.* ELIZABETH *tends the child.*

JAMES: Andrew has left us quite a lot of things . . . Water, salt beef . . . plenty of flour . . . oil for the lamps . . . Aha, here's the axe.

ELIZABETH: Why is it to be a month before he can return to Melbourne?

JAMES: He has to await some material coming in from Portsmouth before he can bring our goods over . . . and also he has to call in to Port Adelaide to put down and pick up . . . Goodness, he's left us enough ball and powder to start a war.

ELIZABETH: I pray we never need to use it.

JAMES: Aye, and we won't if I've got anything to do with it.

[ELIZABETH *puts the child away and searches in a bag.*]

ELIZABETH: I'm glad I brought these spelling and reading books because as soon as the kirk is finished and we've got everything settled, I'll try and organize some sort of social function for our neighbour's children's Sunday school . . .

[JAMES *brings a primitive telescope from the box and surveys the terrain through the glass.*]

JAMES: [*lightly*] Elizabeth, that may be some time. Remember, our nearest neighbours — and by that I mean white neighbours — are about two hundred miles that way. Now, if you're referring to our dark skinned neighbours, they are . . .

[JAMES *starts. Slowly he moves away from the box, his telescope trained on the ridge behind them.* ELIZABETH *moves instinctively to her child.*]

ELIZABETH: James . . . *James*, what is it? Is it . . . the natives?

JAMES: A small number of them . . .

[*There is a flurry of movement behind him. He turns to see* ELIZABETH *searching furiously.*]

Elizabeth, what *are* you doing?

ELIZABETH: I'm looking for the gun . . . Here it is . . . James, help me . . . Don't just stand there.

[JAMES *looks to the ridge, then quickly goes to* ELIZABETH.]

JAMES: Elizabeth, calm down . . . It's going to be alright . . . Everything will be alright . . .

[ELIZABETH *subsides. There is fear in her eyes, but beneath is a clear mind.*]

Elizabeth . . . You alright?

ELIZABETH: Aye, James, I'm alright. Do what you have to do.

JAMES: Listen carefully . . . We must remain calm at all times. On that ridge over there are several native people . . . watching us. Now, I'm going to try and communicate with them.

ELIZABETH: James, don't go too far . . . please. Stay where I can see you.

JAMES: Elizabeth, if we don't go to them . . . they may come to us. Do you understand what I am saying? I'd rather they came to us as friends, not as some war party.

ELIZABETH: Aye, James, I understand.

JAMES: Very well, I'll go then . . .

[*He takes a moment to gather himself. He looks to his wife and son. Their vulnerability inspires him to be resolute.* ELIZABETH *clutches the rifle to her side.*]

Only use that as our very last alternative.

[*He looks to the ridge and slowly walks out to the middle of the clearing. He raises the telescope and slowly scans around the ridges and back again. After a while he lowers the telescope with a sigh of relief.*]

I do believe they've gone.

[*He turns and walks back to the lean-to. His smile of relief disappears as* KOONOWAR, *bedecked in full war dress, steps from behind the tent to stand between him and* ELIZABETH. *His wife starts, but* JAMES *pacifies her with a gesture. He turns to the warlike* KOONOWAR. *The casual spear nestled in the woomera held in front of him belies the speed with which that weapon can pierce a man. The warrior is relaxed and poised. Movements in the background catch* JAMES' *eye, but he looks without moving his head.* ELIZABETH *inches towards the rifle.*]

[*Slowly, deliberately, eyes trained on* KOONOWAR] Elizabeth, don't do it . . . Stay calm . . . whatever you do . . . There's a dozen or more of them . . . You'd get one shot . . . that's all . . . before they speared us with their darts . . . I'll see if he understands any Tahitian . . . [*To* KOONOWAR] *Tia . . . ruha . . . ni . . . aloha.*

[KOONOWAR *answers with a barrage of Boandik. He orders them to leave or suffer the consequences while* JAMES *smiles and nods. The message is clear.*]

ELIZABETH: James?

JAMES: Elizabeth . . . if we are to leave here alive . . . you must trust me . . . Do what I say without question . . . Understand?

ELIZABETH: [*barely audibly*] Aye, James . . . Whatever you say.

JAMES: Very well . . . Leave the rifle and pick Michael up and bring him to me . . . slowly now.

[ELIZABETH *stifles her terror and incomprehension and does as she is bid. As she moves* KOONOWAR *jumps back and brings his spear to bear on the terrified woman.* KOONOWAR's *attack is stopped as* ELIZABETH *gives voice to a hymn.* JAMES *picks up the hymn with gusto. The warrior is taken aback by the actions of these strange people. Fascinated, he watches.*]

Elizabeth . . . keep singing, that's it, my girl . . . Keep
coming.

[ELIZABETH's *voice doesn't falter and she succeeds in totally be-*
wildering the amazed warrior. While KOONOWAR *is distracted,*
ELIZABETH *picks up the baby and moves quickly to her husband's*
side. JAMES *takes the child and slowly raises him as an offering to*
KOONOWAR. *The singing stops abruptly and a heavy silence*
falls. ELIZABETH *reacts, then lowers her head in silent anguish.*
For an eternal moment they are frozen in these attitudes.
KOONOWAR *slowly lowers his spear and tentatively comes for-*
ward. He looks from parents to baby, then grunts and gestures to
his unseen comrades. He approaches the couple in little circling
movements, back and forth, coming and going, till at last he
stands quite close to both JAMES *and* ELIZABETH. *He watches*
JAMES *warily as he puts a hand over the baby. He is surprised,*
then the tension breaks as his chuckle grows to laughter and soon
all three are laughing amid the slowly building babble of
Boandik, Scots and English.]

SCENE SEVEN

The Campbell camp, afternoon. The camp is deserted, and some boxes
and odds and ends lie around. MIRNAT *enters from along the beach look-*
ing out across the sand in front of her. Her dillybag and some food hang
by her side. She also carries her child in a fur bundle. She stops in line
with the camp and, almost without interest, casts a look at the tent. She
coughs, then stands ready for flight. No one comes. Stealthily, she moves
to the tent. Like a nervous animal she reacts to every sound before she
takes each step. She reaches the tent and cautiously looks in. She is spell-
bound by everything: the tent material, ropes and so forth. She silently
comments to her child about each discovery. Her attention is drawn to the
box near the entrance and her fear of the obvious magic of these spirit
people is pretty heady stuff. She stands for some time looking at the array
of objects in the box, then casts a last look around and tentatively puts out
her hand. She touches and immediately withdraws. One can't be too
careful with this spirit stuff. Finally she picks up a small ornate jewel

*box with a ballerina on top. As she moves the lid with a finger the music
starts. She drops it and grabs her child. She stands and sees* ELIZABETH
and her child. Both women anxiously study each other. As ELIZABETH
moves towards the rifle resting on the log, MIRNAT *backs slowly away
towards the beach. On reaching the rifle,* ELIZABETH *cocks the hammer
and slowly brings the rifle to point at* MIRNAT, *who watches, totally
fascinated.* MIRNAT *has no idea about the rifle, and is more interested in
the 'spirit' child. In Boandik she tells* ELIZABETH *that she also has a
baby, and they should look at each other's child.* ELIZABETH *slowly
lowers the gun and both women share the joy of their children.*

SCENE EIGHT

The Koonowar camp, early morning. Currawongs and magpies call.
MIRNAT *cooks the leg of mutton in the coals of a fire.* KOONOWAR *is
fascinated by the meat. He moves about the enclosure.*

MIRNAT: Sit down still somewhere, Koonowar. You make a
    person fidgety.
KOONOWAR: I'm just thinking about that one there. That hair
    is like the *kooramo* possum, but he runs like a dog . . . old
    mirrigan dingo . . . and he sings out . . . like a . . . like this:
        [KOONOWAR *makes a bleating sound.*]
MIRNAT: Were there many?
        [KOONOWAR *nods.*]
    Big mob, eh? Were they hard to catch.
KOONOWAR: Nah. There was a mob of them standing together
    and even when I got up close to them . . . they didn't run
    away . . . They just stood there . . . So when I was about
    from that log there, I planted . . . lay flat on the ground . . .
    Next minute this one . . . he came over to see what I was
    . . . Well . . . he looked down at me . . . like this:
        [*He pulls a face.*]
    And I looked up at him. [*Holding a hand near his face*] And he
    was this close . . . Hey, I got a fright . . . I mean, I thought

he might bite me or something, so I cracked that one with my waddy . . . Poor thing.

MIRNAT: Did you talk *willa bana* with him?

KOONOWAR: Oh, yes. I talked for a long time with him . . . then I rubbed his belly with grass and I called out his name plenty times, let those spirits know we thank him for his meat and we're sorry and all that and how he helps us with food.

MIRNAT: It looks like it's ready . . . Mmm, smells good.

[*They eat the meat in true traditional style using a sharp stone and sharp bone and the old five fingers.*]

KOONOWAR: Those *karato* . . . Y'know, I don't like to mix with them . . . Makes my blood run cold when I think about how they keep changing their skin . . . And you see their eyes? . . . Got no colour, eh? Just like water, eh? What do you say about the *wetjala* white woman?

MIRNAT: She showed me her baby. Oh, it was the same colour as a baby possum . . . *kooramo*. I left some yam and lily root with her and look what she gave me.

[*She collects a small bag and shows the contents to* KOONOWAR: *it is flour.*]

She showed me how she mixes this one with water like we do with *pardhi* . . . That's the bread we got now. Try some. Go on, it's good.

[KOONOWAR *tentatively tastes it, then spits it out. He shakes his head, then grabs the bag and hurls it away. He produces his war club.*]

KOONOWAR: This is *devil food*. Don't you bring this here again or I'll give you this . . .

[*He threatens her with the club.* MIRNAT *cringes humbly.*]

Do you hear me, stupid woman? Don't you ever bring those *karato* things here again and bring their evil things here . . .

[MIRNAT'*s fear of* KOONOWAR *is overcome by greater fear as she backs away and points past him.*]

KOONOWAR: Now don't start trying to get a — . . .

[*He turns to see* VESSY, *a white man, standing with a rifle in one hand and a flintlock pistol in the other.*]

Way . . .

[*The bullocky looks imposing in all-weather moleskin and a great beard bristling under the broad hat.* KOONOWAR's *first reaction is to attack with his club, but he is stopped by the gun pointing at him. He has heard of the white man's lightning stick and stands back watching with alert, lowered eyes. The bullocky places the pistol in his belt, then walks arrogantly over to the leg of mutton and inspects it.*]

VESSY: [*lifting the leg of mutton*] You takem this one. Bad. No bilong you, bilong white man, the *karato* . . . Me bilong law . . . law of the . . . *karato.*

[KOONOWAR *and* MIRNAT *respond to the white man in broken Boandik. As they speak with him, their curiosity overcomes their fears.*]

KOONOWAR: You're speaking our Boandik tongue; where do you come from?

MIRNAT: What is your country?

VESSY: Me? Er . . . me, er . . .

[VESSY *sees* MIRNAT's *interest and seizes his opportunity.*]

Mootatunga man . . .

KOONOWAR: I see . . . I can speak a little Mootatunga . . . We can understand each other. But how is it you're *karato* . . . and a law man, too?

[*Over the following,* VESSY *openly watches the attractive* MIRNAT.]

VESSY: Long time . . . before . . . me lost . . . Big water . . . land of *koodoo* . . .

KOONOWAR: *Koodoo!* . . . The land of the *dead* . . . and you came back?

VESSY: Me come back . . . as *karato* . . . Old Idmanna . . . Mootatunga . . . old woman . . . she see me . . . take me home . . . her lost son return.

[VESSY *watches* MIRNAT *for a moment. Suddenly he points the rifle at* KOONOWAR *and grabs* MIRNAT *with his free hand.*]

[*To* KOONOWAR] Time we go . . . You no makem trouble. You come . . . *karato* law . . . punish you for take this one. Me got this one lightning stick . . . kill you, you try run away . . . okay? You come this way . . . You wait near horse.

[KOONOWAR *goes to challenge the bullocky but is stopped as the rifle barrel is pushed against his chest.* VESSY *pushes* MIRNAT *away and concentrates fully on* KOONOWAR *for the first time. Unseen by* VESSY, MIRNAT *retrieves* KOONOWAR's *war club and approaches the bullocky.*]

Elder of *karato* say to me . . . 'Bring that man who take my jumbuck, bring him to me . . . live . . . or dead.' You hear me, *gamoo?* Me call you bad name . . . eh, *gamoo. 'Gamoo'* bad name, eh? Why you no fight me . . . eh? You fright . . . this lightning stick, eh? Me and your lady . . . we gonna . . . dance . . . eh, woman?

[*The war club arcs down on the head of the unfortunate bullocky. The lights fade to blackout as* KOONOWAR *raises his spear.*]

SCENE NINE

The Campbell camp, evening. The fire is going, and ELIZABETH *sits and knits thoughtfully. She hears* MIRNAT's *approach and looks up, then, by the light of the oil lamp, prepares the evening's lesson books.* MIRNAT *sits, head down.*

MIRNAT: [*murmuring*] *Wona na,* 'Lizbit. [*'Hello, Elizabeth.'*]
ELIZABETH: *Wona na,* Mirnat . . . *Ngat ju* . . . English? [*'Hello, Mirnat. Can you say 'Hello' in English?'*]
MIRNAT: [*with some effort*] Ah . . . low . . . Ul . . . low.
[ELIZABETH *mouths the words with her.*]
Huh . . . Huh . . . Hullo.
ELIZABETH: *Wa bunna,* Mirnat, very good.
[MIRNAT *smiles proudly, then looks around.*]
MIRNAT: *Nga nar bi* . . . Chaym? [*'Where is James?'*]
ELIZABETH: He's gone . . . Adelaide . . . mmm, *wirra* . . . *num.*
[*She attempts to explain in very poor Boandik, but at last reverts to the easier Boandik hand and sign language, translating to herself in English:* JAMES *has gone by boat to send some stores to*

sheep farms on the coast. Before she can finish her explanation she is interrupted by a nearby voice.]

McGUINNESS: Very impressive, I'm sure.

[*Both women instinctively come together. Before them stands a police corporal at attention. He is dusty and his beard gives him the appearance of a Santa, but his eyes belie the goodwill in his appearance.*]

McGUINNESS: Begging your pardon, ma'am, I didn't mean to alarm you. My name is McGuinness . . . Corporal with His Majesty's Royal Mounted Police. I'm here on official business. Might I speak to you and your husband?

ELIZABETH: I'm afraid my husband's away at the moment. Perhaps I may be of assistance. [*With a twinkle in her eye*] Won't you come and sup with us? I am Elizabeth Campbell and this young lady is Mirnat of the local . . . indigene nation.

[ELIZABETH *is fully aware of the effect of her words on the police officer. He remains standing; he doesn't dare look upon* MIRNAT.]

McGUINNESS: Mrs Campbell, it concerns me to see you . . . alone among . . . native people. I cannot understand how Mr Campbell could allow you to be left unprotected . . . These people are savage, primitive people.

ELIZABETH: Corporal, I have more to fear from my own kind, in the form of the riffraff who call themselves men, who prey upon simple defenceless native women . . . like this young woman.

McGUINNESS: Mrs Campbell, I've a long way to travel . . . I've eaten . . . But thanking you for the kind invitation. Briefly, I've been instructed by my superiors to inform you . . . Er, madam, is it wise to speak so publicly?

ELIZABETH: It's quite alright. Mirnat speaks very little English. You may speak quite freely.

McGUINNESS: Very well . . . As I was saying, I've been instructed to warn you of possible skirmishes that may occur in this district between . . . the native population and ourselves. We've had reports of open clashes with insurgents. Cattle have been herded into muddy ground and speared. Sheep speared and carried off. At one camp we

found over fifty carcasses. All this from this coast to along
the Murray River with some of our people brutally killed
by the savages. Our punitive measures have had some
effect in this district, I'm proud to say.

ELIZABETH: Were there many native people . . . captured?

McGUINNESS: Captured?

> [*He smirks, then shows concern.*]

Well, I can tell you I've not lost a prisoner.

ELIZABETH: How many have reached our courts and how
many have been killed out there?

McGUINNESS: They've got the message. You can be sure of
that, ma'am. Now the other reason I'm here is I'm looking
for one of the ringleaders of this area . . . I think they call
him 'Canna . . . wi' or 'Canoa' . . . Something like that. I'd
like to talk to him about the disappearance of a bullock
driver . . . Name of Vessy. About three months ago. Last
believed travelling through this area and hasn't been
sighted since. You haven't seen . . . ?

ELIZABETH: I've not seen a white person whom I haven't
known for three or four months. As for this ringleader, I've
not heard of such a person. Perhaps he comes from an area
close to this. I'm sorry, Corporal, I can't be of more
assistance to you.

McGUINNESS: I'll be on my way, then, ma'am. If I may say so,
ma'am, it's a real pleasure to see our Christian ways reaching to the levels of . . . all manner of men. I'll take my leave,
then, but mind a word of warning: keep both eyes open for
this lot. No matter how well-behaved they appear, mark my
words, they'll turn on ye . . . Bite the hand that feeds them,
they will. I bid ye goodnight, Mrs Campbell.

> [McGUINNESS *leaves, and* ELIZABETH *quietly drinks her tea.*
> MIRNAT *turns to* ELIZABETH *and asks in hand signs if the*
> *policeman is looking for* KOONOWAR.]

ELIZABETH: Yes, Mirnat. The policeman is looking for your
husband.

> [MIRNAT *signs 'Why?'*]

Why? . . . Because a white man is missing . . . Have you
seen any strange white man?

[MIRNAT *goes to the doorway, then turns and gently smiles at her.*]

MIRNAT: G — . . . good . . . night . . . 'Lizbit.

[ELIZABETH *looks quizzically at the departing figure. The lights fade to blackout.*]

SCENE TEN

The Campbell camp, evening. The sea is heard in the background. An earthen stove made from the clay of a giant ants' nest glows in a corner. There is a small oil lamp burning on a table. JAMES *writes in a journal. He studies his work for a while, then stands, stretches and walks to the edge of the tent. He looks out across the dark sea. Off, a horse arrives and is tethered. Heavy footsteps approach.*

JAMES: Who goes there?

McGUINNESS: 'Tis I, Reverend Campbell.

[CORPORAL McGUINNESS *steps into the light. He wears an oilskin all-weather coat.*]

JAMES: Corporal McGuinness. Ye've picked a fine time for calling. Come by the fire. Hot drink?

McGUINNESS: Thanking you. A small one if ye will.

[*He goes and stands by the stove.* JAMES *hands him a warm drink, then clears away his writing.*]

'Tis cold out. I'd sooner be bedded on such a night.

JAMES: Not wishing to be disrespectful, Corporal, but . . . a crow call at night is an ill omen.

McGUINNESS: A discreet analogy, good Reverend . . . and indeed accurate. I may well be the prophet of doom.

JAMES: Indeed. What is your news?

McGUINNESS: Koonowar.

JAMES: What of Koonowar?

McGUINNESS: Some six months ago I came through this area in search of a missing person: a bullocky, 'Vessy' by name. I'd met your good wife on that occasion. When I'd enquired after the whereabouts of one Koonowar . . . although in truth I had not the proper pronunciation at the time, but my enquiry gave a name very similar . . . your good wife unfortunately had no knowledge of the man.

JAMES: An easy misunderstanding, don't you think, Corporal? Two lone women and a stranger out of the night, albeit a law officer.

McGUINNESS: Certainly, good Reverend. Under such circumstances, 'Canoa' or 'Cannawi' could hardly be interpreted as 'Koonowar', could it? Even more strange, I am now led to believe the . . . woman in your wife's company . . . is called 'Mirnat', is she not?

JAMES: Make your point, Corporal.

McGUINNESS: By good fortune I detained a native from this area . . . He was begging on the docks of Port Adelaide. 'Karim' was his name. D'ye know him?

JAMES: Yes, he's a Mootatunga man. Not a very reliable witness, I'm afraid. He's quite deranged. Is it now a crime for native people to walk the streets of our towns?

McGUINNESS: Indeed, no. The natives are seen quite frequently in our Port Adelaide docks area. What caught my attention about Karim was the oversized oilskin overcoat he wore. On closer inspection I noticed it was the type that bullockies wore. When asked where he had got it, he openly replied that a man . . . a very kind man gave it to him during the winter. In fact, I learnt a great deal of things. He spoke of the man's wife, Mirnat, who was a close friend of the local reverend's wife . . . Am I disturbing you, sir?

JAMES: Get on with your game.

McGUINNESS: Oh, you think I'm playing the game, do ye, Reverend? Let me tell you, sir, I am an officer of the law. I'm good at my job. I believe in what the charter of justice stands for. When a man — white, black or yellow . . . or green . . . anyone — breaks the law . . . I will find him and bring him to justice. I'm not the one playing the games. There are people on this land that think they can become judge and jury . . . They may see fit to protect the lawbreaker . . . for whatever reason . . . It is still breaking the law, Reverend. I now have the information I need to bring about an arrest for the leader of the Boandik tribe: . . . Koonowar.

JAMES: What are you wanting of me?

McGUINNESS: I'm deputising men throughout this area to help me capture this man. I'm asking you to join the deputation. With your knowledge of the area . . . and the native people.

JAMES: You once boasted to my wife that your . . . raiding parties never took prisoners. Is that still the case here? How many black prisoners ever reached our courts?

McGUINNESS: A good many, Reverend . . . Quite a good many. I've managed to deliver all my prisoners.

JAMES: What about Slaughter Creek, over there at the Lagoons area? Not one black person was brought in alive.

McGUINNESS: It was an open conflict . . . The whole place was a battlefield.

JAMES: There were women and children among the dead. Your deputies must have shown exceptional courage.

McGUINNESS: I'm sorry to see a man of some intelligence being guided by emotional fervour.

JAMES: White men indiscriminately killing defenceless natives hardly needs a genius to see the white man's scales of justice.

McGUINNESS: Reverend, this is the frontier. Many injustices have happened . . . and undoubtedly will happen in the future. There is not the manpower to uphold the full letter of the law. This land needs men like you . . .

JAMES: No, Corporal. I am unable to accept your kind invitation to the weekend shoot . . . Remember one thing, Corporal. This frontier is opening up. We are all being watched. We are all accountable.

McGUINNESS: I'm sorry you feel that way. I'll take my leave, then . . . And convey my good wishes to your dear wife.

[*He leaves.* JAMES *stands and watches for a time, then turns and goes back to his table, sits and continues to write in his journal. Suddenly he stops, alert, listening for some strange sound. Slowly he pulls a flintlock pistol from the drawer of the table and turns to*

see KOONOWAR, *hungry, tired and hunted. He hand signs to*
JAMES.]

KOONOWAR: Bread . . . bread . . .

> [JAMES *lowers the gun and looks at the emaciated man before
> him. He puts the gun back in the drawer, goes to a side cupboard
> and takes out smoked beef, bread and some dried fruit which he
> serves up to* KOONOWAR. *He offers a seat but* KOONOWAR *sits
> on the ground and eats with gusto.* JAMES *watches discreetly, then
> becomes introspective.*]

JAMES: Aye, my friend. Here we sit for the second time since
we first met that warm autumn evening . . . Eat up, my
friend; this is the least I can do in retribution for the storm
we've brought to your shores. But you're not alone in your
suffering. I've seen more than my share . . . In my country
. . . my people . . . on the Lowlands . . . they were out
fighting in the war . . . against the French; and when they
came back all their lands were lost . . . sold, and they had
to work for the new owners . . . our own people. They were
Scots too! But they were Highlanders . . . They had
money, power, and they forced us off the land, our land.
Just like yours, Koonowar. Land we'd had for generations.
I've seen my people hungry and poor . . . starving in their
own country. Eat up, my brother. I can understand how
you must be feeling. Some of my people joined the British
armies and fought their colonial wars. Them that had
money went to Canada. We who had little or no money . . .
came to Australia.

> [JAMES *walks up and back a little, deep in thought.*]

And what's to become of ye, my man, eh? Fifty lashes or a
hangman's noose . . . or perhaps if they're feeling generous
you might end up with shot in ye . . . dying on ye own land
at least . . .

ELIZABETH: James?

> [JAMES *turns to see* ELIZABETH, *draped in a robe, standing at
> the tent. He silently entreats her to join them. She comes forward
> nervously and nods politely to* KOONOWAR, *who stops eating for
> a moment, then continues.*]

JAMES: The poor devil's near starved to death.

ELIZABETH: How is that possible? They are such good hunters.

JAMES: No doubt there'd be little respite if you're being hunted all over the country.

[JAMES *falls silent and stirs the fire.* ELIZABETH *watches him intently. He sees this.*]

Elizabeth, I can't stand by and watch a fellow human being be hunted down and shot like some kind of wild game. I'll go with him to collect his wife and child and we'll come back here and wait for the Corporal.

ELIZABETH: James, I totally agree with all you say about those hunting parties, but it's all the more reason for not getting too involved . . . Ye canna do much on ye own. One man against fifty . . . probably highly intoxicated . . . oafs. A dangerous combination: . . . liquor and guns. There's no reasoning.

JAMES: I've still got to try, Elizabeth. I couldn't have this man's blood on my hands knowing I did nothing to help him . . . God would never forgive me . . . I would never forgive myself.

[JAMES *goes to the tent and puts on the all-weather coat and hat. He goes to the drawer, opens it and lifts out the pistol. He looks at it, then puts it back. The baby cries a little and* ELIZABETH *goes into the tent.* JAMES *taps* KOONOWAR *on the shoulder and uses hand signs.*]

Koonowar, we go your camp . . . bring Mirnat . . . baby . . . come here, okay?

[KOONOWAR *nods.*]

Alright, Elizabeth, we shouldn't be long. If that Corporal does call again, tell him to wait here with his rabble and we will be here with Koonowar . . . Also, we will be making sure he gets a proper hearing. Is that alright, then, Elizabeth?

[ELIZABETH *comes out of the tent with the baby. She goes up to* JAMES *and kisses him gently on the cheek.* JAMES *smiles, then leaves with* KOONOWAR. *The night sounds close in. Fade to blackout.*]

SCENE ELEVEN

The Koonowar camp, night. MIRNAT *cooks food by the fire. She hears a bird call and answers it.* KOONOWAR *enters. He looks tired and hunted. He smiles and turns as* JAMES *walks in.*

JAMES: *Wo* — . . . *na na*, Mirnat.

MIRNAT: Goot efening, Chayms. Please . . . you come sit here . . . ne' fire.

JAMES: Thank you. I'm here . . . to help Koonowar. *Karato* law man was at my camp. Hunt for Koonowar with plenty guns. I want to stop the . . . er *karato* law man . . . from . . . er, not to hurt Koonowar.

MIRNAT: Me unnastan, Chayms. You make fren' for Koonowar . . . Good. You wait li'l bit . . . Me, Koonowar . . . tok.

KOONOWAR: [*to* MIRNAT] This is a good man, this *karato*. He gave me food. That *karato* law man has been down to the beach looking for me. Two days ago a big mob of *karato* were there with their lightning sticks too. I knew they were looking for me. I was watching them but they didn't see me. They wanted this man to go with them . . . Very strange. He wouldn't go.

MIRNAT: Koonowar, let's go before it's too late. We can go to the bird people in the south . . . or to the big hills over that way to the sunrise.

KOONOWAR: You say it so easily . . . Go where? *This* is my land . . . This is me . . . This land is us . . . Our people are here in these rocks . . . in those waterholes.

MIRNAT: Koonowar, there are places we can go where the *karato* will never find us . . . We can —

KOONOWAR: [*interrupting*] We can do nothing. The *karato* are everywhere and there are more and more coming every day. I have been as far as the great sand hills over there, the land of the Wiradjiri where the sun rises, but there are no men left. They wear the skins of the *karato* and speak with

the loud voice of the *karato*. They live in the hut of the *karato*.
Perhaps that is how it must be . . . perhaps.

[*He rises and walks to the edge of the clearing and looks out.*
JAMES *slowly rises as if listening.* MIRNAT *hears the sound too,
listens and looks around. As* KOONOWAR *speaks, indistinct
voices are heard shouting and laughing.*]

I can remember when I was a boy how I ran over this land.
That big water was where I caught my first fish.

[*Only* KOONOWAR *hears the sounds of his people calling his
name. His eyes search the darkness desperately.*]

KOONOWAR: Here . . . I'm here, Wirawai . . . Dullamon . . .
I'm here.

[MIRNAT *comes up behind* KOONOWAR *and touches him
tenderly. He turns to her, his face aglow with excitement.*]

They're here . . . Our people have come back. I knew they
would. Come on, we got to get the food ready, woman . . .
Come on, my Mirnat, they're going to be real hungry . . .
and we'll show those *karato* . . . We'll show those snake devils
. . . Mirnat, why are you crying? . . . Aha, you're happy,
eh? . . . I feel like crying too, I'm so happy . . .

[MIRNAT *is terribly distraught.* JAMES *comes to her side and
places an arm around her shoulders.* KOONOWAR*'s face becomes
fearsome and he turns.*]

Wait, Mirnat . . . It's not our people . . . It's those *karato*
. . . Quick, hide; don't let them get you . . .

[*The voices in the distance are clearly white men shouting to each
other. There is no escape.* MIRNAT *fetches her son and cradles him
in her arms.* KOONOWAR *and* JAMES *grasp hands. A silent bond
is sealed.* KOONOWAR *is himself again. He kisses his son, looks
at* MIRNAT *and holds her gently, then breaks. He picks up his
spear and war club and turns to* JAMES, *who gently guides*
MIRNAT *away.*]

JAMES: Mirnat . . . Go, take your child and run. Go to
Elizabeth . . . Quickly now . . . Go, my child. God speed.

[MIRNAT *exits.* JAMES *goes to* KOONOWAR.]

I know you can't understand me, my friend, but I will stop
this slaughter before it begins. You wait here.

[*He stops and turns, resigned.*]

If I fail, may God bless us both.

[JAMES *turns and, with arms upraised, marches down the hill like a true Christian.*]

FIRST VOICE: [*off, shouting*] There he is . . . Get him!

SECOND VOICE: [*off, shouting*] There's two of 'em!

[*Suddenly all hell breaks loose. A barrage of gunfire explodes.* KOONOWAR *races to the edge and sees the fallen* JAMES. *He raises his spear and club strongly.*]

KOONOWAR: Here I am . . . I am Koonowar . . . warrior of the Boandik nation . . . I am a man . . . Come and meet me man to man . . . if you dare . . .

[*With a war cry he leaps into the attack. Snap blackout. There is a melee of shouts and gunfire, then all goes deathly quiet. The lone, distant cry of a woman lingers in the air, then silence.*]

END OF ACT ONE

ACT TWO

SCENE ONE

Clarendon House, day. Centrestage stands a podium in a single spot. The crowd — the audience — settles and the MAYOR *enters in full mayoral attire. He goes to the podium, adjusts his glasses and organises his speech papers.*

MAYOR: Your Excellency, Lady Mulray, distinguished guests, ladies and gentlemen, boys and girls. Rarely have I had the opportunity to officiate at such an historic occasion as that which we are witnessing here today, on this Tuesday the twenty-fifth day of November, eighteen sixty-two. This fine building has been chosen for a most just and humane cause. Remnants of a once lost and desolate race of people have been rescued from the brink of extinction. This once proud race were to fall victim to such simple diseases as the common cold. Smallpox also took a terrible toll on these poor simple people . . . But much . . . much more lethal was man's age-old enemy: . . . alcohol. On such simple people this was to prove the most devastating . . . Then, in eighteen forty, on our very own south-east coast, came a ray of hope in the form of a young Christian family. The late Reverend James Campbell, with his lovely young wife, Elizabeth, who is with us here today, began their evangelism among the native people of the area. Anthropological studies were begun with the good reverend and his wife and I believe their son, Michael, has produced some material along those lines. If I might mention here that young Michael lived among the native people from birth until he was about five years old and has continued his association with the native peoples and was recently commended by Governor Grey for his wonderful work in preserving the knowledge of the native people of the area . . . So today we pay tribute to the memory of Reverend Campbell and his work among the . . . [*Referring to his notes*]

Bo . . . wan . . . dik . . . Yes, Boan — . . . dik . . . people
who are to benefit from this man's great work. This building shall house twelve . . . dare I say 'chosen ones'? . . . Yes,
twelve young . . . Boandik girls, and these fortunate young
women shall be house trained and educated in the
domestic skills of our society. Their training shall include
cooking, housekeeping and childminding, so all you good
ladies out there will have a good supply of well-trained
housekeepers and 'nannies'. This fine home, henceforth to
be known as 'Clarendon', which I believe is the birthplace
of the late reverend, shall be a landmark in the history of
our fine town, and will be a reminder of the fine pioneering
stock of our nation. It is with great pleasure and privilege
that I declare Clarendon officially open.

[*The lights fade to blackout.*]

SCENE TWO

ELIZABETH *and* MIRNAT's *loungeroom, evening. The room is lit by a
small light in the corner. The furnishings are simple and sparse with the
odd religious decorations. The door slowly opens and* MICHAEL
CAMPBELL, *a man of some twenty years, enters followed by* DANNY
CANOA, MIRNAT's *son, also twenty. They are well-dressed and in high
spirits — in more ways than one. In their endeavour to remain quiet
they succeed in bumping furniture and giggling.* MICHAEL *shushes*
DANNY *as they weave between furniture. Finally both collapse together
on the lounge and sprawl out.*

MICHAEL: Did you see the look on the Mayor's face?
DANNY: I thought Lady Mulray was going to faint.
MICHAEL: You shouldn't have done it, old son.
DANNY: What?
MICHAEL: You know what you did. We've got to keep those
    people on side. They are very influential people, mate.
    They can make things very difficult for us.

DANNY: I think what we should be doing is try to set up some sort of school, you know? So we can teach our people about things like money and reading and all that sort of thing. I mean, what future is there in our girls housekeeping for some rich white woman?

MICHAEL: That's a great idea, Danny, except for one thing. Our girls aren't interested.

DANNY: What do you mean 'aren't interested'? They've never been asked to do anything else. Anyway, what makes you say that?

MICHAEL: Well, girls are girls, no matter who they are. I mean, what has any of their own men got to offer them? Half of them are always drunk or lounging around the corners begging. And when they do get a woman they keep her pregnant, poor and busted up. Whereas the white blokes, they've got money, they don't knock them around, they treat them like ladies. Now, if you were a woman, which would you go for, eh?

DANNY: I don't know, mate. It's all so . . . pointless. Take me: when I was doing my apprenticeship, every shit job around they gave to me. All the good jobs went to people like Frankie McGuire or Wilfred Nelson, just because they come from good families.

MICHAEL: Well, you've got to be thankful for one thing, mate. There aren't many of your people who have got jobs, let alone become qualified tradesmen. Anyway, McElvoy thinks you're one of his top tradesmen.

[MICHAEL *stands, walks over to the kitchen and pours himself a glass of water from a jug.*]

You know what I think? A couple of smart young blokes like you and me should be seeking our fortunes in Ballarat.

[DANNY *jumps up.*]

DANNY: Gold, gold . . . You're right . . . That's where we should be heading. I mean, it shouldn't be hard to get a licence. Aunt Liz knows the Land Commissioner. We could even afford to get the best equipment with the money we've saved.

MICHAEL: Did you see those Chinese people going through town the other day? Mr O'Brien was telling me he had some through Ballarat from Bendigo on his way back from Melbourne and said that there are hundreds of Chinese people at the diggings.

DANNY: It's amazing that our government lets all these wogs in . . .

MICHAEL: Oh, great . . . You sound really good, Danny . . .

DANNY: What's wrong with you?

MICHAEL: Mate . . . our families have been fighting racism all our lives, so don't you start calling people names because of their race.

DANNY: Ah . . . Mick . . . I was just jokin' . . . I didn't mean anything.

MICHAEL: And neither did Judas.

DANNY: Come on, Mick . . . Stop talkin' so serious . . . Give us a hand wrestle.

[*They clear a little table in front of the lounge and commence an arm wrestle. During the process they knock over the glass. They jump up as the inner door opens and* MIRNAT *enters doing up her dressing gown. Without a word she goes across to the kitchen and opens a cupboard. She takes out a glass and pours herself a drink from the jug, then comes over and sits in a lounge chair.*]

MIRNAT: Alright . . . now you've woken me up . . . tell me about it.

DANNY: Mum . . . you would not believe where we went tonight. Do you know Hathaway's Inn?

MIRNAT: Isn't it that place near the point with the two big lights out front?

DANNY: That's where we were, Mother.

MIRNAT: Bit flash . . . isn't it? . . . How come you were there?

MICHAEL: Well, actually it was my idea, Aunt Mirnat. After we had the official opening, we went with the boys to the Chain and Anchor and had a couple of drinks.

MIRNAT: Alcohol? . . . My, you boys are growing up. What was Hathaway's like?

MICHAEL: The food wasn't bad, but the service was terrible. I would have walked out in the first minutes if it hadn't been for Danny here.

MIRNAT: Oh?

MICHAEL: When we arrived the staff made it quite clear they did not want to have anything to do with us, let alone serve us. I was really offended, but Danny refused to be put off. When a waitress finally came to sit us at a table we were put in a pokey little place in half light —

DANNY: [*interrupting*] Table Zee . . .

MIRNAT: What's that Table Zee?

DANNY: It's the table out in the cellar. But I didn't let that worry us. When I realised what was happening . . . and after a little conference with my brother here . . . we decided we'd like the vacant table by the window near the front, and that's where we went and sat.

MICHAEL: Not without some very disturbing looks from some of the other patrons.

DANNY: Which included such notables as our honourable mayor and his wife and the governor's wife . . . They were all there . . . googly eyed and staring . . . Those very same people who'd been here being so sanctimonious.

MICHAEL: But they had their comeuppance this night.

MIRNAT: Don't know why you want to go somewhere where you're not welcome . . . Can't enjoy yourself like that . . .

MICHAEL: Aunt Mir, I would have, but our friend here was in a very playful mood and you would have been quite impressed with his performance.

MIRNAT: What did you do, Daniel?

DANNY: By the time they managed to feed us, many of the other customers had gone, but the official table was still quite full . . . and so were some of the officials at the table, and when they started to discuss the 'natives', the governor's secretary came over and in a loud voice asked me if I could explain to the officials how one catches wallabies. So . . . I said we need some gum leaves, which the secretary kindly enough went out and got for me. And I told them this very high piercing noise made by the gum leaf stops the wallaby in its tracks. And when we left they were all practicing.

MICHAEL: Fitting justice, I feel, to see all those blue bloods . . . with matching blue faces.

MIRNAT: I'm going to bed, you two.

> [MIRNAT *rises and leaves. The boys follow, laughing and jostling. Fade to blackout.*]

SCENE THREE

ELIZABETH *and* MIRNAT'*s loungeroom, afternoon.* ELIZABETH *hums as she works on a piece of embroidery. She is now in her fifties.* MIRNAT, *also in her fifties, paints a picture of Clarendon as she smokes her clay pipe.*

MIRNAT: Y'know, Elizabeth . . . that old coot . . . Governor Wha'sisname . . . Mulray . . . his speeches get longer and longer the older he gets . . . Lord, my back was aching . . . and the air in that place . . .

ELIZABETH: I was nearly passing out with the heat. Still, it was a nice speech.

MIRNAT: It's a nice crop of oranges this year . . . Yes, I suppose it was a good speech . . . Michael looked good in that new suit y'got him.

ELIZABETH: Where was Danny? I didn't see him at all.

MIRNAT: He was there. Up the back, helping with the lights. He's a real busybody, always sticky-beakin' into everyone's business.

ELIZABETH: What time did they get in last night?

> [MIRNAT *puffs up a smoke screen.*]

MIRNAT: Dunno . . . I heard 'em come in, but don't know what time it was.

ELIZABETH: Has Danny said any more about wanting to go away?

MIRNAT: Well, he's twenty . . . Wants to stretch his wings . . . and he's finished his apprenticeship . . . Nothing to hold him here, really. Suppose there is more chances in the big places like Melbourne . . . Adelaide. I heard Michael talking to Danny about working on a newspaper in Sydney. He getting itchy feet too?

ELIZABETH: He wants to try and get some of his writings published. He mentioned that the *Chronicle* in Sydney is interested in looking at his material. He wants Danny to give him a hand with all he's written about the Boandik.

MIRNAT: Poor thing. Danny wouldn't know too much.

ELIZABETH: You'll be surprised how much Danny remembers. What . . . he would have been . . . six . . . seven years when we moved here . . . Oh, Mirnat, do you remember how wonderful they looked in their wee clothes all muddy and smiling?

[MIRNAT *becomes pensive.*]

MIRNAT: Seems like it was yesterday. Y'know, I felt really bad when I left my country.

ELIZABETH: Mirnat, I never realised you felt that way. I mean you seemed so happy . . . and pleased to be . . . coming with us . . . I mean . . . it was you who kept everyone's spirits up with your stories . . . You were always laughing.

[MIRNAT *looks straight at* ELIZABETH, *who smiles expectantly, the concerned friend.*]

MIRNAT: Listen, Elizabeth . . . I don't think you'll ever be able to understand the blackfella. You'll never know what it's like to see something . . . precious as what our land is to us . . . the Boandik . . . to me. Oh, yes, my friend, I was laughing . . . but that's so my people couldn't see I was bleeding inside. I had to be strong to give them hope . . . It's no matter we lost our home . . . our name . . . everything . . . We had to keep going . . . We had to.

[*The friends sit close. They don't touch, but nevertheless share each other's presence.*]

ELIZABETH: Your name? You've got your name: 'Canoa'.

MIRNAT: That's not our proper name. 'Koonowar' is our name. I take my husband's name.

ELIZABETH: Hold on, Mirnat. When I asked you what name —

MIRNAT: [*interrupting*] You never asked me, Elizabeth. James and you just put that name down 'Canoa'. I didn't know

how to talk good English. No, Elizabeth, you put down that
name.

ELIZABETH: Alright, Mirnat, if that name was so important to
you —

MIRNAT: Course it's important. What if they was to call you
'Cambi' or 'Compill'?

ELIZABETH: Alright, Mirnat.

MIRNAT: Ah, Elizabeth, I didn't mean to upset you.

ELIZABETH: You're not upsetting me! All this carry-on over a
name.

MIRNAT: Elizabeth, in my way, Boandik way, our name has to
be strong, so when my spirit goes to the Dreaming, to the
land of the *koodoo*, it will find its way back to its resting
place. It might be in that old gum tree out the back. You
wouldn't want my spirit to wander about with nowhere to
go, eh? Anyway, if I miss on my Dreaming I'll just go over
to Jesus. I'll have it both ways, eh?

ELIZABETH: Oh, you mad thing. I always felt you were happy
to be . . . safe here with us. I remember those horrid men
coming around with their cheap wine . . . trying to entice
our girls away. Those animals . . . Oh, I shudder when I
think about them. James, bless his soul, could not tolerate
them.

MIRNAT: Poor old James. Remember the time that whaling
boat came in? James was only a skinny fella but boy, he
could fight.

ELIZABETH: He was a bit stubborn. I told him that there was
no real harm done with that fellow.

MIRNAT: No real harm? . . . That sailor was going over the
odds.

ELIZABETH: He was drunk . . . and he just wanted to talk . . .
He wasn't doing anything . . . He was harmless.

MIRNAT: James give him 'harmless' . . . Pow! . . . Fair in the
mainsail. He was a steppy little preacher, our James was.

ELIZABETH: He was a good father . . . to both our boys . . .
Koonowar would have liked James.

MIRNAT: I don't know about that. He had a respect for James,
but he just never trusted white people . . . even you.

ELIZABETH: I can understand that. Heavens, the first time I saw him I thought he was the most ferocious being I'd ever seen in my life. After that first meeting I only ever saw him at a distance whenever he came to meet you after our lessons.

MIRNAT: I tried to show him how to write and he watched me write his name, and when I explained that mark I made in the dirt was him, he rubbed it out with a branch and nearly cracked me with it because he believed that it's like . . . witchcraft. To make a mark about somebody. In the old way if you made a picture or drawing of somebody . . . that's like taking his soul away . . . Those old clever fellas used to just get a bit of hair . . . and they'd somehow put it in clay or something and the man or woman belonging to that hair . . . they'd die because he'd call that person's soul away.

ELIZABETH: Those old superstitions are gone now, Mirnat. You're a Christian now, saved through the grace of our Lord. As Christians we have to save all people from the darkness of ignorance and superstition.

MIRNAT: That's true what you're saying, Elizabeth . . . about ignorance, but superstition is with everyone. I've seen superstitious white people chucking salt over their shoulder . . . and you . . . 'Don't cross those knives' . . . and what about your black cats?

ELIZABETH: Yes . . . well, some bad habits stay around . . . but we still have to fight them, though they may seem harmless enough.

MIRNAT: What? Are you saying that whitefellas' superstitions are alright, but not blackfellas'?

ELIZABETH: I'm saying . . . all . . . black people's superstitions . . . white people's superstitions are bad because they're founded in ignorance and when people are ignorant . . . they can become like animals; their lives are run on instincts . . . like hunger, anger . . . all of man's basic animal instincts . . . My goodness, this conversation is exhausting me. Let's get this fruit in so we can start our preserves. Here's hoping all will turn out well this time, touch wood . . . Oooh.

MIRNAT: Gotcha.

[*The lights fade to blackout.*]

SCENE FOUR

ELIZABETH *and* MIRNAT'*s garden, day. It is deserted.* MICHAEL *enters.*

MICHAEL: [*calling*] Mother! Aunty Mirnat!

[*He goes under low branches and collects an apple. On the way he rubs it against his trousers.* LILLIPA JEFFREY, *a young Aboriginal girl, enters behind him.*]

LILLIPA: If you lookin' for Missus Campbell or Aunty Mirnat, you find'm on the nother side of the house.

MICHAEL: Fine . . . Ta . . . Look, I'm Mrs Campbell's son, Michael. What's your name?

LILLIPA: I'm Lillipa Jeffrey.

[MICHAEL *takes the initiative and shakes hands with the shy girl.*]

MICHAEL: Where are you from, Lillipa?

LILLIPA: I was working at Breezeneath Station . . . before Aunty Mirnat come and get me . . . and bring me here.

MICHAEL: You're coming to live here at Clarendon? That's really good. You'll like it here. Like half an apple?

[*She nods shyly and* MICHAEL *makes small talk while he uses a penknife to cut her a half.*]

Here, let's sit here and eat it.

[*They eat quietly for a while and both exchange little glances.*]

You know, I hate to say it but I think we grow the best apples in the whole of the south-east.

[LILLIPA *laughs shyly. A small silence.*]

LILLIPA: You call out 'Aunty' to Aunty Mirnat . . . How come you . . . ?

MICHAEL: She's not my aunty by . . . the white people's way, but by . . . our . . . her tribal law . . .

    [LILLIPA *takes a mouthful of apple.*]

I'm her son . . . She has another son, Danny.

    [LILLIPA *nods: she knows of* DANNY.]

Oh y'know him. Do y'know what tribe you are?

LILLIPA: Course: I'm Boandik. Aunty Mirnat my real aunty.

MICHAEL: Well . . . I guess that makes us cousins, eh?

    [*Both laugh heartily.*]

LILLIPA: How did you come to know Aunty Mirnat and . . . y'know, all those things . . . ?

MICHAEL: I grew up with Boandik people . . . We used to live at a place we call *Karra Mia Mia*: . . . 'Camp of the Fern-Tree Wattle'.

LILLIPA: Hey, my name mean 'wattle' . . . Sorry, go on.

MICHAEL: Whitefella call it 'Rivoli Bay' . . . '*Karra Mia Mia*' is a better name . . . it's more . . . *wa bunna.*

LILLIPA: Hey . . . you talk Boandik.

MICHAEL: *Mana gamul na wabala wirangy.* [*'If you ask me, whitefella's crazy.'*]

    [LILLIPA *screams with delight.*]

LILLIPA: *Wa bunna* . . . Michael, *Wa bunna* . . . Gee, Michael, you're good.

MICHAEL: I learnt lots of things from the old people . . . I'd been with them for so long . . . I'm Boandik too . . . or as good as being one.

LILLIPA: That's very good, Michael.

    [LILLIPA *beams her approval.*]

MICHAEL: I know that the *karim* lizard is fat now because the *nal a wort* wattle has got flowers . . .

LILLIPA: Bet you can't hunt . . .

MICHAEL: Hey, I'm *koor a na*, the man forest kangaroo . . . When I move about no one can see me . . .

    [MICHAEL *moves to a low hunting stance and moves gracefully over the ground.*]

And when I walk about . . . I can change into anything . . .

    [MICHAEL *mimes a kangaroo scratching.* DANNY *enters. He is a little aggro.*]

DANNY: What d'you think you're doing, Mitch? . . . Stop carrying on like a blackfella. Here some mail for you.

[*The spell is broken.* MICHAEL *is annoyed at* DANNY's *tone, plus the fact that* DANNY *has made him feel guilty about his fondness for the Boandik way of life.*]

MICHAEL: [*aside, to* DANNY] What are you so shitty about?

DANNY: They knocked me back. Ferguson says I'll need another seconder for my application.

MICHAEL: Danny, what do you want to join that club for? They're only a tennis club for Christ's sake. I mean, they're nothing but a bunch of spoilt, arrogant stuffed shirts.

DANNY: You're a member.

MICHAEL: I've only attended one meeting: . . . the day I joined, and that was three years ago . . . I couldn't stand the place.

DANNY: But you're still a member . . . Mitch, you can second my application . . . It's important to me. It's alright for you, mate, you're white . . . Being a blackfella you've gotta mix in the right circles, be in a . . .

[MICHAEL *sees the desperation in* DANNY's *eyes.*]

MICHAEL: Okay . . . alright, mate . . . No real problem. I'll sign the form when we go inside . . . [*Turning to* LILLIPA] Danny . . . I believe you know . . . Lillipa.

DANNY: [*coldly*] Yes. Mitch, you'll come in soon and —

MICHAEL: [*interrupting*] Hold on, mate . . . I didn't hear you . . . even say 'Hello' to Lillipa.

DANNY: I did . . . Mitch, I did . . . You probably didn't hear.

MICHAEL: Yeh, well I'd like to hear it again . . . No . . . No . . . Better still, I want to see you give her a proper Boandik greeting.

DANNY: Don't be such a bloody fool . . . Mitch, I'm very busy . . . and I'm in a hurry.

MICHAEL: What? Too busy to greet one of our own people?

DANNY: She's not your people.

MICHAEL: Okay, she's not my people . . . But she's your people and you better start showing a bit of respect for her . . . instead of trying to play at being a bloody white golliwog.

DANNY: You bloody shit.

MICHAEL: No more pussying around, Danny. I mean it. You show me a proper Boandik greeting with this girl . . . or mate, you can get yourself another seconder . . .

[DANNY *goes cold with anger.*]

I mean it, Danny . . . Your lousy little white tennis club is as important to you as my Boandik culture is to me.

[*Both friends look long at each other. Finally* DANNY *breaks the deadlock. He takes a deep breath and turns and kneels before* LILLIPA. *She is caught unawares.* DANNY *looks up, then takes her hands and puts them on his shoulders. Slowly she rubs her cheeks against each side of* DANNY'*s face, then sits back.* DANNY *rises, dusts his knees and smiles.*]

DANNY: That okay, Michael old son? I'll wait for you in the drawing room.

[DANNY *saunters off.* MICHAEL *comes and sits beside* LILLIPA.]

LILLIPA: It's alright, Michael. I understand my poor brother Danny . . . He's lost in this land. One minute he want to be blackfella . . . next he want to be whitefella . . . Very sad.

MICHAEL: Sometimes I don't know what I want to be.

LILLIPA: Come on, Michael, don't be sad . . . Read your letter . . . Make you feel better, eh?

[MICHAEL *opens the letter and reads. Suddenly he leaps to his feet with excitement.*]

MICHAEL: A publisher . . . in Melbourne . . . They want to print . . . my work . . . Lillipa . . . for years my family have written down the history and the life of your people . . . the Boandik . . . and now they want to make a book . . .

LILLIPA: Oh, Michael . . . that's lovely . . . Good on you.

[*In their excitement they embrace, then realise what they are doing and step apart. There is a moment of embarrassment.* LILLIPA *takes the initiative.*]

LILLIPA: If you're such a good hunter . . . how do you catch a . . . wild duck, eh?

MICHAEL: Duck? . . . Ha, that's easy . . . First of all you go down by the side of the waterhole.

LILLIPA: What about the snakes?

MICHAEL: Ah, you just flick them out of the way, now stop interrupting . . . Back to the ducks. Well, you get down by the bank and you start digging a trench . . . about so big and about so long . . .

LILLIPA: What if you haven't got a digging stick?

MICHAEL: Hey, will you stop butting in? . . .

[*They laugh easily in each other's company. Fade to blackout.*]

SCENE FIVE

A publisher's office, day. MISS MURCHISON, *a well-dressed lady, sits at a desk writing. There is a polite knock on the door.* MICHAEL *enters dressed in a neat suit.* MISS MURCHISON *rises.*

MISS MURCHISON: Ah, you must be Mr Campbell.

[*They shake hands.*]

My name is Miss Murchison. Won't you take a seat? Can I pour you a cool drink? It's so hot in Melbourne this time of the year.

MICHAEL: Yes, I'd like that, thank you.

[MICHAEL *takes in the plush office as the lady fills and brings him a glass of cordial.*]

Thanks.

[*He is aware of her eyes on him as they drink. She puts her glass down and becomes the friendly host.*]

MISS MURCHISON: Well now, you must tell me how one so young has been able to accumulate so much knowledge of such . . . primitive people.

MICHAEL: Actually I lived for the most part of my earlier years with the Boandik people and . . . I'm sorry if in my writings I convey an impression that they are primitive people . . . because in fact you'll find they're quite sophisticated in many respects . . .

[MISS MURCHISON *laughs.*]

MISS MURCHISON: Oh, really, Mr Campbell . . . How clever. You are quite funny . . .

MICHAEL: Hold on, Miss Murchison . . . I wasn't trying to be funny. These people have philosophies which are parallel to any of the great European philosophers.

MISS MURCHISON: Oh, come now, Mr Campbell. You can't be serious.

MICHAEL: But I am . . . I'm very serious. If you'll just give me a moment, I'll show you some examples . . . I wrote two chapters on that very subject.

[*The lady rises from her chair and goes to look out the window. She turns to him.*]

MISS MURCHISON: Mr Campbell, I have read your document with interest. Much of what you've observed has been very . . . very informative . . . about the people . . . Very interesting indeed. Would you come over here for a moment? . . . Let me show you something . . .

[MICHAEL *goes over to the desk where* MISS MURCHISON *shows him some art work and layouts.*]

Do you know what these are, Mr Campbell?

[MICHAEL *studies them for a moment.*]

MICHAEL: They're advertisements . . . for books and magazines.

MISS MURCHISON: Exactly. They are from companies who sent their advertising along to magazines and . . . publishing houses like this one and they pay quite a lot of money to have their notices in our publications. Do you know what would happen if this company didn't receive any of this advertising money?

MICHAEL: You'd probably have to print less books.

MISS MURCHISON: No, my dear boy . . . We'd be finished . . . No more . . . *Fini.*

MICHAEL: Well, that's very interesting . . . but what has that to do with me?

MISS MURCHISON: Everything, Mr Campbell. You see, the board of this company is very sensitive to public opinion . . . as are the advertising companies, and if the public doesn't like something . . . then the advertisers don't like it either. At the present moment the subject of your material isn't . . . popular. Frankly, it's a little too academic. The readers we have are ordinary people off the street . . . We feel that your material wouldn't have much appeal . . . Do you see what I'm trying to show you?

[MICHAEL *sits with his head down. When he looks up he is straining to control his disappointment.*]

MICHAEL: I am amazed at the sort of games you people play . . .

MISS MURCHISON: Mr Campbell. This has nothing to do with your skill as a writer . . . You are quite good . . . In fact, I was going to make an alternative offer to you.

MICHAEL: Oh really? I'd be very interested to hear it.

MISS MURCHISON: I'm so glad you see reason. I knew from the moment I saw you that you were a go-getter. Now, my idea is this: I believe there is very little interest in talking about the native or primitive cultures as such . . . About how they live and what they eat . . . You know . . . But I believe readers would love to hear about their stories of their myths and legends . . . Oh, I think the readers would love their campfire stories of the bush and the animals . . .

[MICHAEL *goes to the door.*]

Mr Campbell, where are you going?

[MICHAEL *turns.*]

MICHAEL: Miss Murchison, I couldn't possibly degrade a culture that has ethics which your culture could not even comprehend.

MISS MURCHISON: Hold on, Mr Campbell . . . I don't understand.

MICHAEL: What happened to Mr Owens? He seemed very happy with my work.

MISS MURCHISON: Mr Owens no longer works for the company.

MICHAEL: Alright, that's fine . . . when good men walk away.

MISS MURCHISON: I beg your pardon . . .

MICHAEL: I'd just like to say this, lady. My parents didn't spend their lives trying to help preserve the knowledge of a culture that has survived aeons . . . for the likes of vultures like you.

MISS MURCHISON: How dare you . . .

MICHAEL: They're not invisible, Miss Murchison. You may

think so and people of your ilk, but they are very much
flesh and bone and their story will be heard.
[*As* MICHAEL *speaks,* MISS MURCHISON *rants and raves about
police and prosecution, but* MICHAEL *shouts louder.*]
You may try and stop it . . . your children . . . and their
children . . . but one day I promise you . . . the world will
hear the name 'Boandik' and they will know . . . *They will
know!*
[MICHAEL *exits and slams the door. A picture crashes to the floor.
Fade to blackout.*]

SCENE SIX

The hospital workshop, day. DANNY *and several tradesmen are dressed
in carpenters' aprons and dust cap, and are covered in wood dust.*
DANNY *works on a cupboard top on which he puts the finishing touches.*
McELVOY *enters. He is clean by comparison with the tradesmen. A
couple of carpenters carry a plank of wood past.*

McELVOY: Danny, can ya jus' hold that fer a minute?
DANNY: Mr McElvoy?
McELVOY: I'll be wanting ye to clean out the archives store —
DANNY: [*interrupting*] Mr Mac, I'm in the middle of this.
Doctor McBean . . . I promised him this week.
McELVOY: And so you'll finish it by the week. In the meantime
I need ya over at archives —
DANNY: [*interrupting*] Mr Mac . . . what's wrong with
McAlister or Buscoe . . . I saw them relaxing out there in
the grounds.
McELVOY: They're already over there . . . working.
DANNY: So why do I have to —
McELVOY: [*interrupting*] Canoa . . . I'll have no more talk . . .
Get ye out and over there and not another word.
[DANNY *fumes as he puts away his tools and takes off his apron.
He heads for the door.*]
McELVOY: Danny. Come back here for a second.

[DANNY *comes back and sulkily looks out the window.*]
What's up, mate?

[DANNY *walks away and tries to express himself.*]

DANNY: My application for the Tennis Club has come to another snag.

McELVOY: Oh?

DANNY: They said Michael's seconder is not good enough because his membership has lapsed. Mr Mac, you're still a member aren't ya?

McELVOY: Used to be. I haven't got time now for all those social graces. Tell me, Danny, what's so important about the club? . . . It's not that McCauley girl you've been seeing, is it?

DANNY: Well, yeh . . . sorta. Mary wants us to play on Saturdays, when she's free.

McELVOY: Ye don't have to join the club to hire their courts.

DANNY: Well . . . it's just that . . . all her . . . people are members and she wants me to become a member. Seeing her dad is on the board and all.

McELVOY: I see. A bit of social climbing, is it?

DANNY: Don't laugh at me Mr Mac . . . Please don't laugh at me!

McELVOY: Alright, son . . . Calm down. I'm sorry. Okay, so the club is going to . . . get you in . . . Do you think *they'll* let you forget . . . you're a blackfella?

DANNY: Well they'd have to be blind not to notice.

McELVOY: That's not what I'm talking about. Look, son, from the time I first set eyes on you I thought, 'This is a different sort of blackfella. He's not going to go walkabout . . . or lay about the docks drunk . . . No, he's gonna make something of himself.' I still believe that . . . You have a lot goin' for ya . . . but ya've gotta run in races that you've got a chance of winnin'.

DANNY: What are ya sayin' Mr Mac?

McELVOY: I wish I was wrong, son . . . but I don't think you'll ever be a member of that club.

DANNY: Ah, get out, McElvoy . . . I've got as much right as anybody of being a member.

McELVOY: That club is for the silvertails, my son. Landed
gentry . . . money people. It's not for the likes of you and
me. Let me show you something.
   [McELVOY *goes to a drawer of the workshop and produces a card
   and a letter from a bundle of papers. He hands it to* DANNY, *who
   reads it quickly.* DANNY *looks up incredulously.*]
DANNY: They . . . knocked you back on your next
application?
McELVOY: Read that there '. . . due to your financial un-
certainty . . .' I was earning twice as much as their
manager. What d'ya say to that?
DANNY: It's not fair . . . It's just not fair.
McELVOY: Neither is a blackfella's bum.
   [*They both laugh.* McELVOY *looks earnestly at* DANNY.]
McELVOY: Son, I've got a lot of time for you and I want you to
win. Now, I'm gonna say something that you might think is
none of my business, but I'm sayin' it anyway because I'd
like you to think of me as a friend. Forget the club. Forget
about Mary McCauley. You *can* get to a stage where you
can be a member of any club . . . and you can marry any
woman ya want . . . black, white or indifferent, but that
time is not now. You're not strong enough yet . . . Ya
haven't learnt enough. Why do ya think I'm always giving
you the hard jobs . . . the dirty jobs? . . . Because I want to
toughen you up, son. You're like . . . unique. There isn't
another black man on this land who has your standing in
this community. You're the only blackfella master builder I
know. Believe me, Danny, I know what these bastards will
do to you if you go playing in their yard. Go when you can
meet them on your terms . . . alright, son? You better get
over to the archives now.
   [DANNY *walks thoughtfully to the door, then turns in mid stride.*]
DANNY: Mr Mac, I'm only a junior master builder . . . at the
moment.
McELVOY: That's bloody right . . . an' don't you forget it . . .
Now buzz off before I dock ya for nagging time.
   [DANNY *exits with a smile. The lights fade to blackout.*]

SCENE SEVEN

The garden, late afternoon. ELIZABETH *and* MIRNAT *prune and clean near the fruit trees.*

MIRNAT: How's Michael coming from the inn?

ELIZABETH: He'll probably come with Mr Waters when he brings the mail around.

MIRNAT: It's nice, isn't it? Our Michael getting his book done finally, y'know, after all these years . . . He really deserve . . .

> [*She is arrested by the sight of a very inebriated* DANNY. MIRNAT *frowns.* ELIZABETH *turns.*]

ELIZABETH: Daniel . . . you're . . .

DANNY: Yes, Aunty E — . . . liz-a-beth, I am quite . . . intoxicated . . . Hello, Mother. You are both probably wondering why . . . I'm . . . like I am.

MIRNAT: Daniel, don't you think you —

DANNY: [*interrupting*] No. I don't think I should . . . do anything in this house . . . ever ..

MIRNAT: Daniel, I think you'd better . . .

> [DANNY *suddenly erupts.*]

DANNY: [*shouting*] Stop telling me what to do . . . !

> [*His outburst shocks even himself.*]

[*Softly*] Just stop . . . Please . . . Nobody tell me what to do . . . Please . . . You've done enough damage . . . Both of you.

> [*He laughs hollowly.*]

You look so shocked . . . Both of you . . . but of course . . . how are you to know how miserable you've made my life, eh? I can still hear those words: . . . 'Keep your mind on the job' . . . 'Put your shoulder to the wheel.' Not one person gave one teeny weeny little thought . . . about what I want in life . . . about what I thought . . . or felt. You all had me believing that white was right . . . the white way is the right way. It's alright if you are white . . . like Michael . . . my white brother Michael: . . . confident . . . successful . . .

an author. And what am I? Eh? I'll tell you what I am: . . .
his little black shadow . . . God, I loved that brother of
mine . . . but he's like you, Aunty 'Lizbit. He's a *karato*: . . .
the snake people. Do you know my dear Aunty 'Lizbit, they
wouldn't even let me into their lousy little tennis club?

ELIZABETH: Oh, Daniel . . . let's go and talk quietly inside . . .

DANNY: What's wrong, Aunt? . . . Afraid the neighbours
might start waving a finger? . . . 'Look', they'll say. 'I told
you those natives were no good . . . Let's get them . . . Yes,
let's put a little strychnine in their flour . . . Let's poison
their water holes . . .'

MIRNAT: Daniel! Stop talking so ridiculous —

DANNY: [*interrupting*] 'Ridiculous' . . . Yes, that's what it is: . . .
ridiculous. These are supposed to be peace times . . . [*Indicating* ELIZABETH] These are supposed to be civilized
people . . . We're supposed to be the savages . . . [*To*
ELIZABETH] Yet none of my people have been the savages
. . . the barbarians that your people are . . . You white
people have declared war on my people, but you're not
doing it out in the open . . . like men . . . Oh, no . . . It's a
sneaky snivelling war . . . a war of worms that slither
around and poison poor gentle people whose only wrong
was they were on land that the worms needed.

[DANNY *pulls some papers from his shirt.*]

Here . . . Read . . . They fell out of an old cupboard in the
old stores at the hospital, when we were cleaning up . . .
Here: . . . a report of poisoned bodies of Aboriginal people
. . . Traces of strychnine found in flour . . . found in water
holes . . . No charges laid . . .

[*With an anguished cry* DANNY *picks up a reaping hook. His
eyes are crazed. The women clutch each other as* DANNY *circles
them. He speaks in an unnatural voice.*]

If your mob want war . . . they'll get it . . .

MIRNAT: Daniel, my son . . . please listen . . .

DANNY: And you . . . you poor thing . . . you believe everything they tell you, don't you . . . ?

MIRNAT: [*reaching to him*] Daniel . . . I love you, my son . . .

DANNY: Don't touch me . . . Please, don't touch me. Why? Why did you bring me here? I have never been happy here . . . I've been so miserable. Why didn't you just let me die at birth . . . there with my father? [*Screaming*] Koonowar!

[*He goes crashing down the path at a wild run.* MIRNAT *tries to follow, but* ELIZABETH *grabs and holds her as* DANNY'*s cries disappear in the distance. The lights fade to blackout.*]

SCENE EIGHT

ELIZABETH *and* MIRNAT'*s loungeroom, evening. The room is barely lit.* ELIZABETH *and* MIRNAT *sit waiting. All is quiet. Suddenly, footsteps approach the door. Both women suddenly brandish weapons and wait. The door handle slowly turns and the door opens. The women raise their weapons as the lights go on.* MICHAEL *stares at them in surprise.*

ELIZABETH: Michael!
MIRNAT: Michael!
[*The women drop their weapons and rush upon him, pouring out their news.*]
ELIZABETH: Michael . . . Michael . . . he's gone mad . . . We were in the garden . . . Going to cut us to ribbons . . .
MIRNAT: My poor boy, he gone real *wirangy* . . . I thought he was going to kill us . . . Oh, Michael, you should have seen his eyes . . .
MICHAEL: Hold on . . . Hold on . . . Calm down . . . Mother . . . Aunt, will you . . . *Quiet!*
[*Both women step away from him and go to each other, afraid that another son may have gone the same way. It may be catching.*]
Mother, I didn't mean to raise my voice . . . Aunt Mirnat . . . I didn't mean to frighten you . . . Here, let's sit down and I'll get us a cup of tea and you can both tell me about it . . . Alright?
[*The women subside.* MICHAEL *tosses off his coat and goes to the*

kitchen. He puts on the kettle and sets out some crockery, then comes and sits in a chair facing them.]

Alright, now. Who wants to start?

MIRNAT: Let me, Elizabeth. [*To* MICHAEL] You know how Danny has been acting strange, lately . . . all moody and biting everyone's head off . . . gritting his teeth all the time. Today at work, he found some papers from the hospital about . . . how somebody was doing these terrible things . . . Oh, Michael, it was terrible . . .

[MIRNAT *cries and leaves the room.* ELIZABETH *sees her to the door, then returns to an inquisitive* MICHAEL.]

ELIZABETH: Some horrid persons are . . . have been . . . poisoning the native people . . . with strychnine.

MICHAEL: What? Are you sure?

ELIZABETH: It's true. It's all in those papers over there.

[MICHAEL *goes to the papers and reads. He is horrified and walks to the window. He has to support himself against the wall. Long pause.*]

MICHAEL: Mother. I can't promise that this sort of thing isn't happening. I've heard rumours of such things, but . . . I didn't believe . . . No, I chose not to believe that this was happening. We are cultured men . . . We aren't animals . . . We couldn't act like savages . . . yet my eyes and ears tell me different. I see hungry . . . beings feeding on the weak of this land, daily growing fat and bloated from the misfortune of simple, gentle people. Yes, we are to blame, we learned, cultured men who brought this scourge to the Boandik people. Yes, we are to blame.

ELIZABETH: Michael, how can you say that? We can't be guilty of such things . . . We . . .

MICHAEL: We are as guilty as the persons who pressed the first trigger . . . who laid out the first bait of poison . . . We are implicated, Mother, by the greatest sin of all: . . . the sin of omission. Let me tell of something that happened when I went to Port Adelaide. I would have been about thirteen. After disembarking, we were walking along the waterway when we saw a crowd of people. In their midst was a large man, a fierce, foul-mouthed bully . . . a bullocky who was whipping this Chinese man. Before I knew what had happened, a man had pushed his way in and placed himself between the man on the ground and the bullocky. I truly believed that bullocky was going to strike him when suddenly he was joined by a man . . . and then another and very soon there was quite a number standing before the bullocky. The oaf made an unseemly remark and walked off. The Chinese man wanted to give the man a reward of . . . could have been gold, but the man bid him a safe journey and went on his way.

ELIZABETH: You never mentioned that to me . . . and you always told me everything. How is it . . . ?

MICHAEL: I suppose I was waiting . . . till the opportunity arose . . . like now.

[*The kettle boils.* ELIZABETH *sits quietly as* MICHAEL *makes the tea and brings it over. They sit for a beat and sip tea.*]

ELIZABETH: They rejected your work, didn't they? . . . Don't look so surprised. I do know my son. You'd have heralded your success from the street.

MICHAEL: Well, soothsayer Mother, I may be down on one knee, but I'm not out . . . Mark my words, I'll see these works published before I'm through. Now tell me about Danny. What happened?

ELIZABETH: He came home this afternoon very inebriated and shouting and ranting like a lunatic . . .

MICHAEL: Danny . . . our Danny . . . drunk? . . . Lunatic?

ELIZABETH: Danny was very drunk. He was upset about some club . . .

MICHAEL: Yes, I know about that one.

ELIZABETH: And apparently he felt he was being made a fool of at work because he kept talking about marrying a white girl . . . silly notions like that.

MICHAEL: That's not a silly notion for Danny to marry a white girl . . . I mean, if they love each other.

ELIZABETH: There's a bit more to marriage than love, Michael. There's a good many things . . . like . . . and stop raising your eyebrows and being so smug; you know what I mean: security . . . a home . . . a good job. All of that.

MICHAEL: Alright, we won't get into that for the moment. So what happened?

ELIZABETH: He accused me . . . us of all being part of the whole conspiracy, and that Aunt Mirnat . . . He said she knew all about . . . white people . . . and should have ended his life there with his father. He was terribly unhappy and . . . quite strange.

MICHAEL: Wonder where he could have gone . . . Maybe he's over at Raymond's place cooling off.

[MICHAEL *puts on his coat and feels something in his pocket. He looks sheepishly at* ELIZABETH *as he shows her a little gift box containing a gold chain and locket.*]

It's just a little something I bought for Lillipa. Hope she likes it . . .

[ELIZABETH *picks up her tea and moves towards the kitchen. She is strangely quiet.*]

What is it, Mother? What . . . Is it Lillipa? Is something wrong with Lillipa? . . .

[MICHAEL *moves quickly across the room to the stairs, but is frozen in his tracks by his mother's tone.*]

ELIZABETH: Michael. She's not there.

[MICHAEL *slowly returns.*]

Aunt Mirnat and I discussed the matter at some length and we decided that . . . it would be better for all concerned if . . . Lillipa were staying elsewhere. We found a very good home for her.

MICHAEL: You both decided . . .? Aunt Mirnat . . . and you?

ELIZABETH: Well . . . I felt it was necessary that . . . you both shouldn't see too much of each other. Michael, I was thinking of your career and your position in this town . . . You couldn't ruin all that . . . for a . . . a . . . an infatuation . . .

MICHAEL: [*quietly*] Where is she? . . . Mother?

ELIZABETH: She's quite a ways from here by now, I should think. More tea, Michael?

MICHAEL: [*shouting*] *Mother!*

ELIZABETH: Don't you dare raise your voice to me, young man!

MICHAEL: You have no right to interfere . . . no one. I will choose my friends. Lillipa is a friend . . . a dear, lovely person and we're friends . . . Just friends . . . but . . . if we should have wanted to become more . . .

ELIZABETH: Stop talking such nonsense. You hardly know the girl.

MICHAEL: And I'm not likely to, either . . . Oh, yes, I see it all now. At first I suspected . . . You don't want me to have relationships . . .

ELIZABETH: Stop being so coarse, Michael.

MICHAEL: Alright . . . Having an . . . affinity with a black girl, but no . . . You don't want me to know any girl . . . unless she has good breeding . . . good schooling. Oh, yes, and above all else . . . has the right connections . . . Well, I'll tell you what I think about all that . . .

MIRNAT: *Michael!* . . .

[MIRNAT *stands at the door.* MICHAEL *stands still and silent as* MIRNAT *comes up behind him.*]

Don't say any more, son. We've all hurt each other enough tonight.

MICHAEL: But how could you do it, Aunt Mir? . . . You of all people . . . you should have understood . . .

MIRNAT: She's not strong like you, Michael . . . She's fragile. You might want to be a friend . . . She will want more . . . Then what could you offer her, eh, son? . . . A good home? Yes . . . A good husband? . . . Yes . . . perhaps, but what about friends, eh? She'd only have you . . . She'd be locked in like a bird in a cage. That little girl is like a butterfly . . . She wants to taste all the flowers in the garden. She doesn't know life . . . Don't do that to her. Don't try and save every drowning creature you meet . . . You've given her a bit of sunshine . . . She take it with her for the rest of her life and she'll always remember you as that little bit of sunshine in her life. As for you, my son . . . you've got a long road and you've chosen to carry a big load: . . . man's injustice . . . That's a big load. Trouble with that one is it picks up more on the way . . . and it'll get heavier, till one day it will crush you . . . or you'll chuck it off your back . . . Then you'll be

like everyone else, only carry little bits of the load . . . fight
a bit of injustice here . . . bit there . . . so you can keep
going in this life.

> [MICHAEL *turns and holds* MIRNAT *to him.* ELIZABETH *touches
> them both.*]

MICHAEL: Sometimes I don't know whether I love you or hate
you, you old *mulluna.*

> [*A call comes from outside.* MICHAEL *crosses to the window. The
> women react as though it is* DANNY. MICHAEL *talks to the caller,
> then returns.*]

It was one of the boys. Danny's down at the docks.

ELIZABETH: The docks . . . That horrible place.

MICHAEL: I'll go get him and bring him home.

> [*He goes to the door, then feels in his pockets. He returns to*
> MIRNAT. *With a wink he hands her the little gift.*]

Will you make sure Lillipa gets this . . . as a going-away
present. I won't be long.

> [MICHAEL *exits.* ELIZABETH *sits in the chair and* MIRNAT *goes
> to her.* ELIZABETH *rests her head on* MIRNAT. MIRNAT *strokes*
> ELIZABETH'*s hair and looks out. In the distance, the mopoke
> calls. The lights fade to blackout.*]

SCENE NINE

---

*A dark alley, night. It is menacingly still. A figure staggers around the
corner into the light. It is* DANNY, *now a little more sober. He is grubby
and untidy. He has been running and puffs as he drinks from a bottle.*

DANNY: I'm going to show those *karato* I'm more than they
bargained for. Know you not I am a warrior . . . a fighting
man. We fought to the death. That's why . . . that's why
. . . there are no more of us left.

> [*He crumples against the wall and slips down to the ground,
> lamenting the fate of his race. Slowly he comes out of the mood as
> he hears the approach of running feet. A girl bursts onto the scene.
> It is* LILLIPA.]

LILLIPA: Danny . . . I'm glad I found you . . . Quick, you gotta come with me . . . Quick now.

[*She tries to help him, but he throws her off.*]

DANNY: Don't touch me . . . you . . . *gamoo.*

LILLIPA: Danny, I want to help you. Big mob of men coming looking for you . . . They got sticks and wood . . . and some got knives . . . They sayin' they gonna catch you and they gonna kill ya for what you done . . .

DANNY: Kill me? . . . *Kill me?* . . . *Me?* . . . Danny Canoa? . . . Ha, they can't even find me, let alone kill me. Anyway . . . what's it got to do with you?

LILLIPA: My brother . . . we are the same . . . you and me . . . We are Boandik . . . We gotta stick together . . .

DANNY: Don't give me that . . . *yarmidja.* Where's your white boyfriend . . . Michael?

LILLIPA: Danny, don't talk about your friend like that. He loves you like a brother.

DANNY: Love . . . Love, ha. Who do you think you're talking to? I grew up with those . . . *karato* . . . I know their every thought . . . I know their way . . . their every move.

[*He laughs.*]

You'd know how they move, eh little Boandik?

LILLIPA: Can you hear yourself, eh? My brother? You all twisted up inside . . . You can't even see straight. You don't even know who your friends are . . . who your enemies . . . You're sick, my brother . . .

[*Suddenly enraged,* DANNY *leaps up beside her and grabs her in a powerful grip. She remains defiant.*]

Go on, why don't you hit me, eh? Come on, brother, that's how you keep your women in place, isn't it?

DANNY: Shut your mouth . . . you . . . tramp. Good enough for the *karato*, eh? . . . Yeh, good enough for the white boys. Take what they want . . . don't they? Black boys not good enough, eh?

LILLIPA: Danny . . . if you want me . . . I'll go with you . . . Danny, do you hear me? I'll go with you now . . . You'll be my first . . .

[DANNY *throws her off and explodes. Even this girl thinks he's a fool.*]

DANNY: Liar . . . Dirty . . . filthy liar . . . You whore . . . harlot . . . You and Campbell have been . . . Don't lie to me . . .

LILLIPA: Danny . . . Michael is your very very best friend. He's my friend. He never touch me . . . No man ever touch me . . . If you don't believe me, find out for yourself. Come on, but we gotta go away from here straight away . . . okay? Quick, Danny, them fellas are coming.

DANNY: Why would you do that, eh? . . . For me? What're you after, eh?

LILLIPA: Danny, my brother . . . we the only ones left. We the only Boandik left. No matter what I feel . . . or what you feel . . . we gotta stay together . . . You and me . . . Keep our blood going, my brother.

DANNY: Stop calling me 'brother' . . . You make it sound like incest.

LILLIPA: We gotta go now . . . Come on, I'll stay with you all night . . . I'll show you . . . You'll be my first man . . . Quick, Danny, we gotta go.

[*Suddenly there is a noise in the alleyway.* LILLIPA *pleads with* DANNY *to go.*]

DANNY: Go on, get off with ya . . . First man, hah . . . You must think I'm stupid . . . Go on, get away with you, ya black bitch, go off with ya white boy . . . Go on, get!

[DANNY *strikes her and she smarts from the slap. Her eyes blaze momentarily, then proudly she turns and slowly walks away and disappears around the corner.*]

[*Calling after her*] Hope you don't have too many dalmatians.

[*He laughs cruelly. He picks up his bottle and takes a drink.*]

First man . . . What a lie . . . a barefaced lie, hah. The bitch.

MICHAEL: She's probably telling the truth, Danny.

[DANNY *swings around to see a figure against the wall in the dark.* DANNY *brandishes the bottle as a weapon.*]

DANNY: Mitch . . . Is that you? . . . Mitch?

MICHAEL: [*almost inaudibly*] Yeh.

DANNY: What are you doing down here? . . . Slumming, eh?

MICHAEL: I've come to take you home, you prawn.

DANNY: Easy on the insults, white boy.

MICHAEL: Boy, you are in a mess, aren't ya? First you smash windows in houses all over the place . . . but setting fire to the clubhouse . . . Boy, you've really stirred up the hornets' nest, y'know.

DANNY: And that's only the start. You and your mob will know what it's like for a change . . . what it's like to see your family torn apart . . . see your families suffer.

[*He takes a swig from the bottle.*]

MICHAEL: Try not to dirty her name with your tongue.

DANNY: Who's that? . . . That whore of yours? . . . Lillipa the wattle? Lillipa the white man's bed mate. Don't make me laugh . . . Campbell . . . I've watched you two over these last few days . . . babbling away in corners. It's pathetic . . . It's sick . . . Still, most white men couldn't pass a young sixteen-year-old, especially if she's black.

MICHAEL: *Ja mulu . . . gammo.* [*'You're an evil slug.'*]

DANNY: I warn you, white boy. Don't you insult me . . . anymore . . . understand?

MICHAEL: What she said is true. I haven't put a hand on her . . . and I believe her. She was offering her most precious gift. Pity it was wasted on a poisoned little rat.

[DANNY *screams painfully and pulls* MICHAEL *out into the alley.* MICHAEL *falls and* DANNY *goes to attack him when he suddenly realises that* MICHAEL *is covered in blood. He looks through bleary eyes at the damage of the knife wounds.*]

You stirred them up . . . alright, Danny. The one thing . . . colonials hate worse than a nigger . . . is a nigger lover.

[DANNY *is beside himself as he flounders for direction. He cries in his terror.*]

DANNY: I'll go get a doctor . . . Mitch, don't you die on me, you shit . . . Wait here, cobber.

[MICHAEL *grabs him in a vice-like grip.*]

MICHAEL: Danny . . . it's too late . . . My friend, don't leave me. Stay with me a little, brother . . . Phew . . . It's not hurting so much now . . . I can feel it . . . all slipping away.

DANNY: Don't die . . . Please, Mitch . . . I'm sorry . . . So sorry. I'll make it up to you . . . I promise I will . . .

MICHAEL: Hey . . . Come on . . . mate . . . We've had a good run, Danny . . . Just make sure of everyone for us, and the writings: . . . promise me you'll make sure you get them published . . . right?

[DANNY *can only nod. He holds* MICHAEL'S *hands to him desperately.*]

Hey, Dan . . . did you see the sunset tonight?

[DANNY *only mumbles.*]

It was like a sheet . . . of ice . . . A red sheet of ice. God, it was . . . beautiful. Hey, Danny, listen . . . I can hear voices.

[DANNY *slowly raises his head and looks down the alley at the audience. Slowly he rises, still holding* MICHAEL'S *hand. he reaches for the bottle.*]

Danny . . . it's singin' . . . It's Boandik . . . Danny, our mob have come . . . We're right, mate . . .

[DANNY *positions himself for an alley fight. He takes off his jacket and wraps it round one forearm.*]

DANNY: Knives it is, gentlemen . . . That's just fine . . .

[*He holds the bottle in one hand.*]

MICHAEL: Danny, listen . . . [*Singing*]
> Oh warinor . . .
> Bina warinor.

Sing, Danny . . . Come on sing, mate . . . Our people are here . . . [*Singing*]
> Oh warinor . . .
> Bina warinor . . .

[DANNY, *at the ready, touches his friend as he sings.*]

DANNY: [*to the mob*] Come on . . . We are Boandik warriors . . . Come and get us . . . if you can.
[*Singing*]
> Oh warinor . . .
> Bina warinor . . .

[*Lights fade to blackout.*]

SCENE TEN

Darkness. The sounds of the Federation celebration. A single spot illuminates a podium, centre stage. ELIZABETH, *now in her eighties, moves to the podium. There is applause. She waits for it to subside.*

ELIZABETH: Your Excellency, all distinguished persons . . . friends. My heart would wish that I might address you at length . . . but alas my bones insist that I be brief. On this auspicious occasion of the creation of our new nation, a federation of Australian states, my colleague and I would like to mention this day heralds the sixtieth anniversary of our Aboriginal girls' college . . . Clarendon. This college has been instrumental in launching the careers of many of our girls into the field of domestic sciences, where many are gainfully employed. We have seen the building of this new nation and we have seen the price paid by the first Australians. These humble people have paid dearly and one day we may celebrate their achievements in the sciences without the 'domestic'. Before I introduce my friend and companion, may I point out that there is a slight error in the programme. The next speaker is Mirnat Koonowar. 'Canoa', I apologise, is a very poor white man's rendition of 'Koonowar'.
  [MIRNAT *enters and takes* ELIZABETH's *place at the podium.*]
MIRNAT: *Nga bara wirrin, baja . . . mulpa.* I think that covers everybody. Good day. [*Exchanging glances with* ELIZABETH] My name is 'Mirnat Koonowar', which translated means 'black swan of the bulrushes'. From that hill over there at that place called Bulli Murra, if you were to cast your eyes around as far as the eyes can, you will see what is the land of the Boandik. I say 'is' because in Boandik law as long as the land is there, so is the law. It's like putting your mark on water: . . . you can put all the lines you want . . . you never change it. It stays the same way. So it is with the land. Man or animal or plant . . . comes and goes. Some foolish men believe they can own the land, but to the Earth Spirit . . . it

is like a flea that tries to own the dog. The law of this land, the Boandik law, says that all is there to use. It will feed you, clothe you . . . protect you and it will be your friend if you learn its ways and live with it. If you don't, it will be your enemy. A man who walked on water said the same thing. I notice that he and the Boandik suffered similar fates. I better go now, but before I do, let me say something to you. This land is alive. It moves, it breathes . . . we know because we are its *keepers*.

THE END

GLOSSARY

BOODOO, penis
BOONTHA, to fall over on your back
COOLAMON, an all-purpose bark or wooden carrier for water, food, or babies
GUNYAH, a bark shelter
GAMOO, an insult
JUMBUCK, a sheep
KEIL, a water hen
KARATO, a snake
KOODOO, land of the dead
KOORAMO, a possum
MOOGADA, foolish, stupid (an affectionate term)
MULLANA, mad person
MUNTER, a kind of apple
MIRRIGAN, dingo
MOPOKE, a bird
PARDHI, seed
WIRANGY, mad
WALIM, spirit people
WETJALA, white person
YARMIDJA, mad, silly

Biographies

JACK DAVIS was born in Perth in 1917 and brought up at Yarloop and the Moore River Native Settlement. He first began to learn the language and culture of his people, the Nyoongarah of the South West of Western Australia, while living on the Brookton Aboriginal Reserve. He later worked as a stockman in the North-West which brought him into contact with tribal society.

He became an activist on behalf of his people and from 1967-71 was director of the Aboriginal Centre in Perth. In 1971 he became the first chairman of the Aboriginal Lands Trust in W.A. and from 1972-77 was managing editor of the Aboriginal Publications Foundation. He is a member of the Institute of Aboriginal Studies in Canberra and has established a course for Aboriginal writers at Murdoch University. He is also a member of the Aboriginal Arts Board of the Australia Council.

His first full-length play, *Kullark*, a documentary on the history of Aboriginals in W.A. was first presented in 1979. It was followed by *The Dreamers* (1983), *No Sugar* for the 1985 Festival of Perth and *Honey Spot*, a children's play. In 1986 *No Sugar* was re-mounted by the Australian Elizabethan Theatre Trust for a season at the World Theatre Festival in Vancouver.

For services to his people Jack Davis received the British Empire Medal in 1977; in 1985 he became a member of the

Order of Australia, received the Sidney Myer Performing Arts Award, an Hon. D.Litt. from Murdoch University and was elected Citizen of the Year in W.A. In 1988, his latest play *Barungin* (*Smell the Wind*) was presented at the Perth and Adelaide Arts Festivals.

EVA JOHNSON was born in 1946 and belongs to the Malak Malak people of Australia's Northern Territory. In addition to being a playwright, Eva Johnson is a feminist, political activist, travelling performer and speaker. In 1981 *Faded Genes* was presented and in the same year, she played the lead role in *Zamisdat* for the Troupe Theatre, Adelaide. In 1984 Eva Johnson wrote directed and acted in *Tjinderella*, part of the First Aboriginal Women's Art Festival. She became Aboriginal Artist of the Year in 1984, and in 1987 *Murras* was workshopped at the National Black Playwrights Conference, and in 1988, was presented at the Adelaide Fringe Festival. Also in 1988, Johnson attended the first International Women Playwrights Conference in Buffalo, U.S.A.

RICHARD WALLEY is an experienced director, designer, actor, musician, dancer and choreographer. His numerous stage appearances include the W.A. Theatre Company productions of *A Fortunate Life*, *The Dreamers*, and *No Sugar* which also toured to the 1987 World Theatre Expo in Canada; and *Bullie's House* presented in New Haven, U.S.A. He founded the Middar Aboriginal Dance Company and has toured with the Company to many international events including the United Nations Concert in Geneva, the Olympic Promotions in Los Angeles and the Rhiesen Fair in Hamburg. Richard has worked on radio and television in the U.S.A., the U.K., Canada and Denmark. He also appeared in the TV series *A Fortunate Life*.

BOB MAZA has worked extensively as an actor, director, playwright and as a consultant in theatre, radio, film and television. He was one of the original members of the Black Theatre in the early 1970's with the production *Basically Black*.

His other theatre credits include *Are You Now or Have You Ever Been*, *Bullies House* and *Clouds*, all at the Nimrod Theatre and *The Cakeman* for the Black Theatre. His plays include *Tiddalik* and *Rain for Christmas* for children's television and *Mereki* commissioned by Toe Truck Theatre. Bob has appeared in most of the television series made in Australia in the past twenty years and also in the mini series *Women of the Sun*, and *White Man's Legend* for the ABC and *Rainbow Serpent* for SBS-TV. His film appearances include *The Chant of Jimmy Blacksmith* and *The Fringe Dwellers*.

JUSTINE SAUNDERS has worked as an actor in theatre, film, T.V. and radio for the past fifteen years, throughout Australia and in America. She also teaches and lectures on acting and Black theatre, and is currently one of five directors of the Aboriginal National Theatre Trust. She was the Artistic Director of the Second National Black Playwrights Conference held in Sydney in January, 1989.

Also from Currency

JACK DAVIS — Barungin (Smell the Wind)

Completing the trilogy *The First Born* which commenced with *The Dreamers* and continued with *No Sugar*, this play addresses the land rights issue and black deaths in custody through the experience of one family. The play is written with Jack Davis' usual honesty and humour.

HYLLUS MARIS and SONIA BORG — Women of the Sun

Four television dramas each dealing with a different time in the two hundred years since white settlement in Australia. The chief protagonist in each drama is a women and the resilience of these women in the face of despair and destruction gives a fresh insight into the history of race relations.

For a complete list of titles with Aboriginal themes contact your bookseller or
Currency Press
330 Oxford Street
Paddington NSW 2021
Tel. 332 1300